A YEAR OF PRAYER

A YEAR OF
Prayer

DAILY MOMENTS OF CONTEMPLATION, DEVOTION & GRACE

STEFANIE ROUSE, MMFT   CALEB ROUSE, MED

ROCKRIDGE PRESS

To our parents, Ed and Sue Stack and John and Kay Rouse:
Thank you for the foundation of prayer you installed in us.
We are grateful for you, admire you, and love you beyond words.

Interior and Cover Designer: Angela Navarra
Art Producer: Tom Hood
Editor: Olivia Bartz
Production Manager: Michael Kay

Photography by Stefanie & Caleb Rouse
Illustrations used under license from Creative Market.

Paperback ISBN: 978-1-63807-759-6 | eBook ISBN: 978-1-63807-624-7
R0

Contents

Introduction

Jesus is calling us to know His heart more intimately. The Holy Spirit whispers to us to slow down as we read His words. God speaks to us, allowing our perspective to be more aligned with His own. Our Mighty Counselor keeps wooing our hearts in prayer and drawing us close to His presence.

I (Stefanie) have had a love for Jesus since I was a child, but my life did a 180-degree turn when I surrendered my life fully to Him during my junior year of college. I experience God's love firsthand and keep seeing His redemption in my life. And I (Caleb) have loved God all my life, but when my lifelong dream of playing basketball was taken from me by an injury during my senior year of college, it rocked me. Jesus is healing both of our hearts and giving us renewed vision for our lives.

We work full-time on our online and writing ministry together. It's our honor to proclaim the gospel, build up relationships, and travel the world shining God's amazing light. Our marriage, ministry, purpose, and relationships have been built on the foundation of prayer. Talking to our Heavenly Father saves each of these areas of our lives. Prayer for us is talking to our best friend, and with it, we get to see God's hand moving in wondrous ways.

This book is broken up by monthly themes to help you grow in some of the most important areas of God's heart. It's set up to help you establish a daily prayer practice, and it offers a variety of interactive and reflective entries.

The Meditations help you slow down to allow His precious words deeper in your heart.

Prayer Prompts help you grow in faith and love for God, others, and yourself.

Affirmations help you claim a simple and short truth throughout your day, bringing God's peace and calmness over your heart.

The End of the Month Practice helps you put into action the refreshed vision of Jesus, to love others out of His abundance of grace.

We pray peace, joy, and love flow through your life as you grow in relationship with your Savior. Our hope is that you not just rush through the pages but allow God's precious words to fill your heart. We pray Jesus will speak to your identity, your situation, your purpose, your life, and your heart right at this moment. We hope you find this book to be a daily source of support, guidance, and deeper assurance that Jesus hears you. He cares about you. He loves you. And He wants to talk with you. Prayer is our most powerful weapon to fight against evil and the way we can directly intercede to change the world.

JANUARY

LOVE

1
JANUARY

"And so we know and rely on the love God has for us. God is love. Whoever lives in love lives in God, and God in them."

1 JOHN 4:16, NIV

MEDITATION

1. Find a quiet and peaceful place to sit.
2. Slow your thoughts and allow your body to rest in tranquility.
3. Take a deep breath in.
4. As you exhale, let your worries, pains, and struggles release from your mind and body.
5. In a gentle whisper, ask God to meet you right here and now.
6. Placing your hands faceup on your knees, receive His love for you.
7. With each breath, silently repeat, "Lord, I receive your love."
8. Closing your hands in prayer, tell God how much you love Him.

2

"Jesus replied: 'Love the Lord your God with all your heart and with all your soul and with all your mind. This is the first and greatest commandment. And the second is like it: 'Love your neighbor as yourself.'"

MATTHEW 22:37–39, NIV

AFFIRMATION

Christ's love covers me like a blanket, so the warmth that fills my soul can spread to the neighbors I encounter today.

3
JANUARY

"See what great love the Father has lavished on us, that we should be called children of God! And that is what we are!"

1 JOHN 3:1, NIV

AFFIRMATION

God loves me so much that He calls me His child.

4
JANUARY

PRAYER PROMPT

Jesus, thanks for always being available to spend time with me. This week, help me spend quality time with you, as well as quality time with important others in my life.

5

JANUARY

"Because of the Lord's great love we are not consumed,
for his compassions never fail. They are new every
morning; great is your faithfulness."

LAMENTATIONS 3:22–23, NIV

MEDITATION

1. Wherever you are, stand and lift your hands to the sky.
2. Silently pray: "Great is your love."
3. As you breathe in and out, feel God's love pouring over you like rain.
4. As you let your hands come down, cover your heart and let the love of the Father fill you with love, joy, and peace.
5. Being filled, allow His presence to flow throughout your body.
6. Feel the warm, inviting, and caring presence of His love for you.
7. Open your eyes and walk into your day wrapped with the power of His love.

6

"I have loved you with an everlasting love;
I have drawn you with unfailing kindness."

JEREMIAH 31:3, NIV

AFFIRMATION

*God's love for me never ends. His kindness
toward me will never fail.*

7

JANUARY

PRAYER PROMPT

Pray for your closest loved ones. Ask God to cover them with His
love today.

8

JANUARY

"For as high as the heavens are above the earth, so great is his love for those who fear him; as far as the east is from the west, so far he removed our transgressions from us."

PSALM 103:11–12, NIV

MEDITATION

1. Let your body fully relax in quiet peacefulness.
2. Bring your hands together in prayer and begin taking deep breaths.
3. With every inhale, silently repeat, "As high as the heavens."
4. With every exhale, silently repeat, "So is your love for me."
5. Slowly take your hands from prayer and stretch your arms out to your sides as far as you can.
6. Now with every inhale, quietly say, "As far as the east is from the west."
7. With every exhale, quietly say, "So far you removed my sins."

9

JANUARY

"The Lord your God is with you, the Mighty Warrior who saves. He will take great delight in you; in his love he will no longer rebuke you but will rejoice over you with singing."

ZEPHANIAH 3:17, NIV

AFFIRMATION

God delights and rejoices over us, His children.

10

JANUARY

PRAYER PROMPT

Dear God, thank you for loving me no matter what has happened in my past, what is transpiring now, and what will take place in the future.

11
JANUARY

> "For God so loved the world that he gave his one and only Son, that whoever believes in him shall not perish but have eternal life."

JOHN 3:16, NIV

MEDITATION

1. Close your eyes as you picture our planet. Think of all the trees, animals, oceans, and people. Imagine a time-lapse video of all the people who have lived on this planet.
2. Now imagine God telling you He brought Jesus to this world out of His love for *you.*
3. Although there are many people, He sees *you.*
4. Imagine Jesus telling you that He loves you so much that He died for you.
5. Breathe out any feelings of failure because He took those feelings on the cross for you.
6. Breathe in His sacrificial love for you and for the world.

12
JANUARY

Dear Jesus, it's hard to comprehend that you love me so much you died for me. Help me receive your love even in the places it's been hardest to receive.

13
JANUARY

"But the fruit of the Spirit is love, joy, peace, forbearance, kindness, goodness, faithfulness, gentleness, and self-control."

GALATIANS 5:22–23, NIV

AFFIRMATION

Holy Spirit, how blessed am I to share in the fruits of your love!

14
JANUARY

PRAYER PROMPT

Jesus, will you help me see others, and myself, out of your eyes of love and forgiveness today?

15
JANUARY

PRAYER PROMPT

Heavenly Father, it says in your word that you are love. Please empower me to say words of affirmation that speak worth over the people's lives I encounter today, so they feel loved and valued for who they are.

16
JANUARY

"Very rarely will anyone die for a righteous person, though
for a good person someone might possibly dare to die.
But God demonstrates his own love for us in this:
While we were still sinners, Christ died for us."

ROMANS 5:7–8, NIV

AFFIRMATION

*Jesus took my place, washes me clean,
and sets me free.*

17
JANUARY

PRAYER PROMPT

Holy Spirit, thank you for your foundation of love. Help me show
love through giving a gift of kindness to a stranger today.

18

"I am the vine; you are the branches. If you remain
in me and I in you, you will bear much fruit; apart
from me you can do nothing."

JOHN 15:5, NIV

MEDITATION

1. As you take a deep breath in, picture yourself sitting next to Jesus under a beautiful fruit tree.
2. As you breathe out, release tension in your body as you imagine the fruit tree growing taller, stronger, and with more fruit.
3. Visualize Jesus telling you that's what your life is like when you stay connected to Him.
4. Picture the roots going deep, receiving nutrients from His love, joy, and peace.
5. Feel the striving leaving your body. Allow the connection to His love to be your source of strength. Tell Him: "Apart from you I can do nothing."

19

JANUARY

PRAYER PROMPT

Dear Jesus, please give me a spirit of love, goodness, faithfulness, gentleness, and self-discipline so I can love others with your love today.

20

JANUARY

"As the Father has loved me, so have I loved you. Now remain in my love. If you keep my commands, you will remain in my love, just as I have kept my Father's commands and remain in his love."

JOHN 15:9–10, NIV

AFFIRMATION

I will love my neighbors like Jesus does.

21

JANUARY

"My command is this: Love each other as I have loved you. Greater love has no one than this: to lay down one's life for one's friends. You are my friends if you do what I command."

JOHN 15:12–14, NIV

AFFIRMATION

*Jesus is the greatest friend
I could ever ask for.*

22

JANUARY

PRAYER PROMPT

Lord, let me show thoughtful affection for my loved ones today.

23

"Love is patient, love is kind. It does not envy,
it does not boast, it is not proud. It does not dishonor
others, it is not self-seeking, it is not easily angered,
it keeps no record of wrongs. Love does not delight
in evil but rejoices with the truth. It always protects,
always trusts, always hopes, always perseveres."

1 CORINTHIANS 13:4–7, NIV

MEDITATION

1. As you let your body relax and take deep breaths, read the scripture above again, but this time replace the word *love* or *it* with God, Jesus, or the Holy Spirit.
2. Picture Jesus telling you how this is who He is for you.
3. Hear God whisper how much He loves you and is protecting you.
4. Visualize the Holy Spirit filling you up with a love that produces good in your life and the lives of others.

24

JANUARY

"…And I pray that you, being rooted and established in love, may have power, together with all the Lord's holy people, to grasp how wide and long and high and deep is the love of Christ, and to know this love that surpasses knowledge—that you may be filled to the measure of all the fullness of God."

EPHESIANS 3:17–19, NIV

AFFIRMATION

Christ's love is more than enough to fill me today.

25

JANUARY

PRAYER PROMPT

I pray for those who feel lonely and afraid, that they can experience God's closeness today.

26

JANUARY

"Your righteousness is like the highest mountains, your justice like the great deep. You, Lord, preserve both people and animals. How priceless is your unfailing love, O God! People take refuge in the shadow of your wings."

PSALM 36:6–7, NIV

AFFIRMATION

God's love is a constant source of shelter.

27
JANUARY

Jesus, I pray for _____ (a person or group of people). They need your love so desperately just like I do, Lord.

28
JANUARY

"For Christ's love compels us, because we are convinced that one died for all, and therefore all died. And he died for all, that those who live should no longer live for themselves but for him who died for them and was raised again."

2 CORINTHIANS 5:14–15, NIV

AFFIRMATION

I can love others because of the overflow of God's love for me.

29

"But because of his great love for us, God, who is rich in mercy,
made us alive with Christ even when we were dead
in transgressions—it is by grace you have been saved."

EPHESIANS 2:4–5, NIV

MEDITATION

1. Find a place to take a peaceful walk.
2. As you walk, take in the presence of God around you.
3. Allow your senses to detect sights, smells, noises, tastes, and textures.
4. With each breath, experience a sense of gratitude for your life.
5. Quietly thank God for making all things new, for creating all things special and unique.
6. At the end of your walk, say to God, "Thank you for your great love today. I feel so grateful for your amazing grace over my life."

30

JANUARY

PRAYER PROMPT

Dear God, help me show acts of service to someone I encounter today. I pray for those who need help from Christians, that we be generous with our time, money, and resources.

31

JANUARY

END OF THE MONTH PRACTICE

The People in Your Life. Who might need a tangible reminder of love? Think of a way you could encourage someone with the truth of God's love for them. Maybe it's paying them a compliment, maybe it's praying for them, maybe it's giving them a hug while saying, "You are loved!" Going out of your way to love others will encourage them and instill a great sense of gratitude and love in your own life.

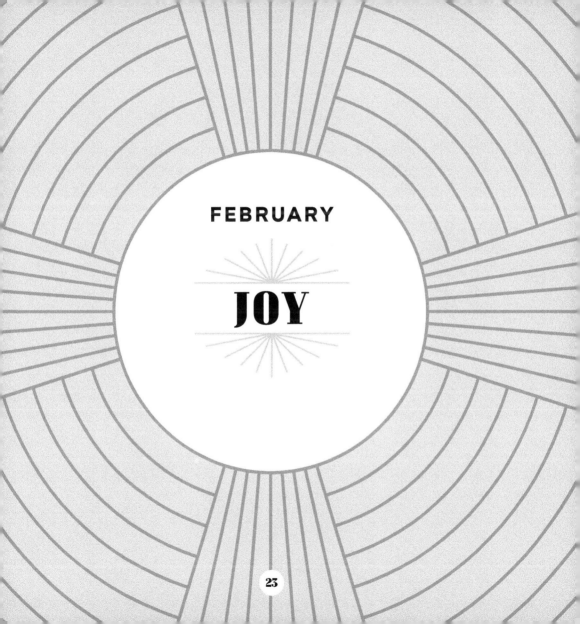

FEBRUARY

JOY

1

FEBRUARY

"You have made known to me the paths of life;
you will fill me with joy in your presence."

ACTS 2:28, NIV

MEDITATION

1. Close your eyes and ask God to join you in a spirit of joy.
2. While receiving His joy over you, smile and think of an instance when He gave you unexpected joy in your life.
3. Allow yourself to sit in that moment with God, absorbing all the joy that comes from His goodness.
4. Receive the joy of the Lord in your heart, in your mind, and in your soul.
5. Pour out any prayers to Him and listen to what He has to say.

2

FEBRUARY

"You make known to me the path of life; you will
fill me with joy in your presence, with eternal
pleasures at your right hand."

PSALM 16:11, NIV

AFFIRMATION

God knows my path, and I am filled with joy in His plan.

3

FEBRUARY

PRAYER PROMPT

Dear God, no matter what circumstances or trials I encounter
today, I will choose to find joy in your presence.

4

> "For the kingdom of God is not a matter of eating
> and drinking but of righteousness and peace
> and joy in the Holy Spirit."

ROMANS 14:17, NIV

MEDITATION

1. Bow your head and close your eyes.
2. Bring your hands to prayer and ask the Holy Spirit to meet you in this moment.
3. Give the Holy Spirit the space to speak and to fill the atmosphere around you with His presence.
4. Inhale the Spirit, and exhale your worries, troubles, and fears.
5. In the calm that is His presence, allow yourself to smile, laugh, or even cry.
6. Let your emotions express the tenderness of what He is speaking over you.
7. Say to yourself, "Righteousness, peace, and joy in the Holy Spirit. Amen."

5

"The Lord is my strength and my shield; my heart trusts in him, and he helps me. My heart leaps for joy, and with my song I praise him."

PSALM 28:7, NIV

AFFIRMATION

The Lord is my strength and my shield. My trusting heart rejoices in Him.

6

PRAYER PROMPT

Today, I pray for those going through difficult times, and ask that God fill them with the joy that comes from being in His presence. I pray that He provides for them today.

7

"As the Father has loved me, so have I loved you.
Now remain in my love. If you keep my commands,
you will remain in my love, just as I have kept my
Father's commands and remain in his love. I have
told you this so that my joy may be in you and that
your joy may be complete."

JOHN 15:9–11, NIV

MEDITATION

1. Find a quiet place.
2. Invite God to fill the room with His presence.
3. Recite the verse out loud or silently to yourself.
4. Now read the scripture again, but this time insert your name wherever it says *you.*
5. Receive these words as if Jesus were speaking directly to you.
6. Let His words penetrate you to the deepest places of your heart and soul.

8

"So with you: Now is your time of grief, but I will see you again and you will rejoice, and no one will take away your joy."

JOHN 16:22, NIV

AFFIRMATION

I rejoice in Jesus; no one can take away my joy.

9

FEBRUARY

PRAYER PROMPT

God, I thank you for _____ (a blessing in your life).
Because of this, I find so much joy in you.

10

"Though you have not seen him, you love him;
and even though you do not see him now, you believe
in him and are filled with an inexpressible and glorious joy,
for you are receiving the end result of your faith,
the salvation of your souls."

1 PETER 1:8–9, NIV

MEDITATION

1. Find a peaceful space to read the verse.
2. Although you can't see Jesus, picture Him with you.
3. His love is more real than the air you breathe.
4. Imagine God's joy filling up your lungs as you inhale.
5. Let all your worries and shame leave your body as you exhale.
6. Contemplate the joy that comes in knowing the salvation of your soul.

11

FEBRUARY

"You turned my wailing into dancing; you removed my sackcloth and clothed me with joy."

PSALM 30:11, NIV

AFFIRMATION

One day, Jesus will wipe away all our tears. He is in the business of exchanging my mourning for dancing.

12

FEBRUARY

PRAYER PROMPT

Dear Jesus, I would love to share your joy with someone I see today. Can you help me?

13

"Though the fig tree does not bud and there are no grapes
on the vines, though the olive crop fails and the fields
produce no food, though there are no sheep in the pen
and no cattle in the stalls, yet I will rejoice in the Lord,
I will be joyful in God my Savior."

HABAKKUK 3:17–18, NIV

MEDITATION

1. Invite the Holy Spirit into this special time.
2. Tell Jesus about a difficult circumstance you're facing, and say, "I will still rejoice in you, Lord. I will take joy in the God of my salvation."
3. Repeat the words until you feel them in your soul.
4. When a negative thought comes up throughout your day, repeat the words of truth over in your heart and mind again.

14
FEBRUARY

"In him our hearts rejoice, for we trust in his holy name."

PSALM 33:21, NIV

AFFIRMATION

Today, I will set all my troubles aside and allow my heart to rejoice in the trusting and abiding love God has for me.

15
FEBRUARY

PRAYER PROMPT

Father, a close relationship with you is full of joy. Will you help me recognize the moments of joy, and pause with me today to soak them up? Amen.

16
FEBRUARY

"Therefore, since we are surrounded by such a great
cloud of witnesses, let us throw off everything that
hinders and the sin that so easily entangles. And let us
run with perseverance the race marked out for us, fixing
our eyes on Jesus, the pioneer and perfecter of faith.
For the joy set before him he endured the cross, scorning its
shame, and sat down at the right hand of the throne of God."

HEBREWS 12:1–2, NIV

MEDITATION

1. Look up into the sky as if you're looking into Jesus's eyes.
2. His are the kindest, most loving eyes you've ever seen.
3. His smile is a delight.
4. Thank Him for enduring the cross with joy to save you.
5. Picture Him on the throne in heaven, happily making everything that's weighing you down disappear.

17

"You became imitators of us and of the Lord,
for you welcomed the message in the midst of
severe suffering with joy given by the Holy Spirit."

1 THESSALONIANS 1:6, NIV

AFFIRMATION

*I feel encouraged because the Holy Spirit
can give me joy even in my suffering.*

18

FEBRUARY

PRAYER PROMPT

Jesus, let me rejoice in seeing your handiwork in creation today.

19

FEBRUARY

"And on that day they offered great sacrifices,
rejoicing because God had given them great joy.
The women and children also rejoiced. The sound of
rejoicing in Jerusalem could be heard far away."

NEHEMIAH 12:43, NIV

MEDITATION

1. Take a deep breath and allow yourself to relax in God's presence.
2. With each inhale, silently say, "This is the day the Lord has made."
3. With each exhale, silently say, "I will rejoice and be glad today."
4. Repeat this process, letting the joy of the Lord strengthen you with each breath.
5. Close your eyes and place your hands over your heart.
6. Ask God to fill your heart with joy today, allowing you to rest in His presence.

20

"Shout for joy to the Lord, all the earth. Worship the Lord with gladness; come before him with joyful songs."

PSALM 100:1–2, NIV

AFFIRMATION

Today, no matter what happens to me, I will rejoice with gladness, knowing I am saved.

21

FEBRUARY

PRAYER PROMPT

Dear Jesus, I want to share joy with those you put in my path today. Let me smile at others and speak of your goodness.

22
FEBRUARY

"Let all creation rejoice before the Lord, for he comes, he comes to judge the earth. He will judge the world in righteousness and the peoples in his faithfulness."

PSALM 96:13, NIV

AFFIRMATION

All creation shows God's love and joy. I will look for God's hand in all I see and do today, and take delight in Him.

23
FEBRUARY

PRAYER PROMPT

Pray for those who are caught in tough circumstances. Pray that God would fill them with the joy of His presence.

24
FEBRUARY

Pray for a special loved one who brings you joy, that God will fill their day with abundant joy.

25
FEBRUARY

"Consider it pure joy, my brothers and sisters, whenever you face trials of many kinds, because you know that the testing of your faith produces perseverance."

JAMES 1:2–3, NIV

AFFIRMATION

In every trial, I can choose joy, because of the hope I have in Jesus.

26

"You will go out in joy and be led forth in peace;
the mountains and hills will burst into song before you,
and all the trees of the field will clap their hands."

ISAIAH 55:12, NIV

MEDITATION

1. Close your eyes and picture a peaceful meadow around you.
2. This meadow is filled with grass, and there's a light wind blowing.
3. Imagine taking off, running faster than ever before, filled with youthful excitement.
4. Imagine you see Jesus off in the distance. As He calls you over, you run toward Him.
5. As you get close, you feel the warmth of His love as He smiles at you.
6. Ask Him whatever you want, allowing Him to respond to you.
7. Open your eyes and allow the beauty of what you experienced to fill you with joy and peace.

27
FEBRUARY

—

"But let all who take refuge in you be glad; let them
ever sing for joy. Spread your protection over them,
that those who love your name may rejoice in you."

PSALM 5:11, NIV

MEDITATION

1. Sit quietly and allow your mind to slow down.
2. Think of your recent burdens and imagine stacking them up like bricks.
3. Imagine God taking all those bricks of burden from you.
4. In a gentle whisper, say, "God, I take refuge in you."
5. Meditate on this truth and let joy fill your soul.
6. Picture the God of Heaven's Armies being a shelter over your life.
7. Hear God say, "Feel my protection over you today."
8. Tell Jesus: "I rejoice in you. I'm so glad you're my protector."

28

END OF THE MONTH PRACTICE

Choosing Joy, Not Forcing Happiness. Perspective plays a big role in how we see our circumstances. Write out a summary of James 1:2–3 on a Post-it Note or on a mirror: "I consider it a joy to face trouble, because I know the testing of my faith produces perseverance." Repeat it to yourself any time you experience difficulty or are tempted to complain. Trials and joy seem like opposites, yet God's word tells us we can rejoice during suffering. Learn to go to God first. He doesn't want us to force happiness. He wants us to be reassured that if it's not good, then it's not the end of His story for you.

MARCH

PEACE

1

"I have told you these things, so that in me you may have peace. In this world you will have trouble. But take heart!
I have overcome the world!"

JOHN 16:33, NIV

MEDITATION

1. Wherever you are, close your eyes and slow your breathing.
2. Invite the presence of the Holy Spirit to surround you in peace.
3. Now picture the most peaceful place in which you've ever been.
4. Allow yourself to embrace the fullness of the peace that surrounded you in that place.
5. Say to yourself, "In this world I may have troubles."
6. Then whisper, "But Jesus has overcome the world!"
7. Let those words of peace sink in.
8. Allow your mind and body to accept victory, in this moment, through Jesus.

2

"Now may the Lord of peace himself give you peace at all times and in every way. The Lord be with all of you."

2 THESSALONIANS 3:16, NIV

AFFIRMATION

I can always find peace because the Lord is always with me.

3

PRAYER PROMPT

Pray to receive God's peace over every exhausting situation, fear, and unwelcomed worry today.

4

"Humble yourselves, therefore, under God's mighty hand,
that he may lift you up in due time. Cast all of your anxiety
on him because he cares for you."

1 PETER 5:6–7, NIV

AFFIRMATION

*God brings us peace because
of His great love.*

5

"Many, Lord, are asking, 'Who will bring us prosperity?'
Let the light of your face shine on us. Fill my heart with
Joy when their grain and new wine abound. In peace
I will lie down and sleep, for you alone, Lord, make
me dwell in safety."

PSALM 4:6–8, NIV

MEDITATION

1. As you are lying down to sleep for the night, take two deep breaths.
2. With each inhale, say to God, "Let the light of your face shine on me."
3. With each exhale, say to God, "Fill my heart with joy."
4. Close your eyes and slow your breathing further.
5. Exhale, quietly saying, "In peace I will lie down and sleep."
6. Inhale, quietly continuing, "For you alone make me dwell in safety."

6

PRAYER PROMPT

Jesus, shine your light upon me and grant me peace in any unresolved issues I may face today.

7

MARCH

"Great peace have those who love your law,
and nothing can make them stumble."

PSALM 119:165, NIV

AFFIRMATION

*Through God's word, I can stand strong
and bring peace to others.*

8

"Peace I leave with you; my peace I give you. I do not give to you as the world gives. Do not let your hearts be troubled and do not be afraid."

JOHN 14:27, NIV

MEDITATION

1. Relax your mind and body in quiet stillness.
2. Breath in and squeeze your shoulders, arms, and hands tightly, making your body more and more tense.
3. Then release the tension with an exhale, saying, "God, I give you my troubles." Give your troubles and worries over to Him.
4. With your body now relaxed, picture God filling you with His peace.
5. Slowly moving your hands toward your heart, receive the peace God is giving you.
6. Finish by silently saying, "Jesus, I receive your peace; because of you I am not afraid."

9

"But he was pierced for our transgressions, he was
crushed for our iniquities; the punishment that brought
us peace was on him, and by his wounds we are healed."

ISAIAH 53:5, NIV

MEDITATION

1. Picture meeting with Jesus right now in a peaceful setting.
2. He holds out His hands and shows you the holes from being nailed on
   the cross.
3. As you take a deep breath, hear Him tell you: "By my wounds, you are healed,
   sweet child."
4. His eyes look at you with so much love, you know all your past faults are
   wiped away by His blood.
5. Picture all the shame you've ever carried drift away as you receive the abundance of peace, knowing you're fully forgiven.

10
MARCH

"He replied, 'You of little faith, why are you so afraid?'
Then he got up and rebuked the winds and the waves,
and it was completely calm."

MATTHEW 8:26, NIV

MEDITATION

1. Jesus wants to meet with you today.
2. Find a quiet and cozy space.
3. Take a few deep breaths and welcome Him to sit next to you.
4. As you breathe out, imagine exhaling anything you've been afraid of recently.
5. As you inhale, imagine Jesus telling you He can make your storm calm, too.
6. Tell Him any fear you've been holding on to.
7. Imagine Him gently reminding you: "I will walk with you through it all."
8. Picture Jesus calming the waves in your life.

11
MARCH

"Then they cried out to the Lord in their trouble,
and he brought them out of their distress. He stilled the storm to a
whisper; the waves of the sea were hushed."

PSALM 107:28–29, NIV

AFFIRMATION

God can calm any storm.

12
MARCH

PRAYER PROMPT

Dear Jesus, I thank you in advance for calming this storm in my
life: _____ (describe your trouble).

13
MARCH

"Do not be anxious about anything, but in every situation, by prayer and petition, with thanksgiving, present your requests to God. And the peace of God, which transcends all understanding, will guard your hearts and your minds in Christ Jesus."

PHILIPPIANS 4:6–7, NIV

MEDITATION

1. Where in your body do you feel tension today?
2. Take a deep breath and stretch while imagining God's peace entering you, bringing relaxation to your whole body and soul.
3. Look around at what you can see and reflect to Jesus about why you're thankful for different things.
4. Let that thankfulness start to diffuse the tension and bring you peace.
5. Breathe out your worries.
6. Hear Him tell you: "I see you, child, I hear you. I'm working this out."
7. Feel the peace of this truth deeply.

14

MARCH

"You have been a refuge for the poor, a refuge for
the needy in their distress, a shelter from the
storm, and a shade from the heat."

ISAIAH 25:4, NIV

AFFIRMATION

*Jesus is my place of safety
and refuge, always.*

15

MARCH

PRAYER PROMPT

Pray that the hearts of people around the world will be softened,
and that Jesus's peace will be experienced by all.

16
MARCH

"Do not repay evil with evil or insult with insult.
On the contrary, repay evil with blessing, because
to this you were called so that you may inherit a blessing.
For, 'Whoever would love life and see good days must
keep their tongue from evil and their lips from
deceitful speech. They must turn from evil and do good;
they must seek peace and pursue it.'"

1 PETER 3:9–11, NIV

MEDITATION

1. The Holy Spirit wants to help you today.
2. Maybe you've been hurt by someone lately.
3. As you take a deep breath, hand over that pain to God.
4. Picture Jesus reminding you that this person is in His hands.
5. With each inhale, say to yourself, "I will repay evil with a blessing."
6. With each exhale, say to yourself, "You exchange my pain for blessings and peace."

17
MARCH

"Therefore, since we have been justified through faith,
we have peace with God through our Lord Jesus Christ."

ROMANS 5:1, NIV

AFFIRMATION

*I have peace knowing Jesus paid the price for
my mistakes and the mistakes of others.*

18
MARCH

PRAYER PROMPT

Dear Heavenly Father, please help my family in the trials we are
facing, especially _____ .

19
MARCH

Pray this verse to God over your life: "Come to me, all you who are weary and burdened, and I will give you rest. Take my yoke upon you and learn from me, for I am gentle and humble in heart, and you will find rest for your souls."

MATTHEW 11:28–30, NIV

20
MARCH

Strive for full restoration, encourage one another, be of one mind, live in peace. And the God of love and peace will be with you."

2 CORINTHIANS 13:11, NIV

AFFIRMATION

I choose to offer peace.

21

PRAYER PROMPT

Dear Jesus, there's no substitute for your peace. Let me meditate on your truth and be filled with your presence.

22

MARCH

"'The Lord bless you and keep you; the Lord make his face shine on you and be gracious to you; the Lord turn his face toward you and give you peace.'"

NUMBERS 6:24–26, NIV

AFFIRMATION

I am blessed by the Lord. He sees me and gives me peace.

23
MARCH

"How beautiful on the mountains are the feet of those who bring good news, who proclaim peace, who bring good tidings, who proclaim salvation, who say to Zion, 'Your God Reigns!'"

ISAIAH 52:7, NIV

MEDITATION

1. In a quiet place, slow your breathing and become still.
2. Let your body and mind release the stresses and worries of the day.
3. In a soft voice, say, "Jesus reigns. He is my joy and my strength."
4. As you reread Isaiah 52:7, let this thought sink in: "Beautiful are the feet of those who bring good news, who proclaim peace and salvation, and who bring good tidings."
5. Think of one person that you can encourage today with good tidings.
6. With your hands in prayer, place that person into the care of God, and ask Him to bring them peace.

24
MARCH

Jesus, I thank you for these blessings of peace this past
week: ....

25
MARCH

"'Though the mountains be shaken and the hills be
removed, yet my unfailing love for you will not be
shaken nor my covenant of peace be removed,'
says the Lord, who has compassion on you."

ISAIAH 54:10, NIV

AFFIRMATION

*God's compassion and peace
will never leave me.*

26
MARCH

"The Lord replied, 'My Presence will go
with you and I will give you rest.'"

EXODUS 33:14, NIV

MEDITATION

1. Find a quiet place and relax your mind and body.
2. While sitting in the stillness, thank God for His presence in your life and ask Him to reveal a time when He was present with you.
3. Concentrate on how God made himself known to you in that moment.
4. Allow Him to comfort you now. Use your senses to feel His presence around you.
5. In silence, give Him the space to speak to you.
6. Make special note of anything He highlights to you in this moment.
7. Let these words resonate with your spirit: "My presence will go with you and I will give you rest."

27
MARCH

Pray for God to rest His presence on you and give you abundant peace.

28
MARCH

"You will keep in perfect peace those whose minds are steadfast, because they trust in you. Trust in the Lord forever, for the Lord, the Lord himself, is the Rock eternal."

ISAIAH 26:3–4, NIV

AFFIRMATION

When I trust in God, He will keep me in perfect peace.

29
MARCH

"Let the peace of Christ rule in your hearts, since as members of one body you were called to peace. And be thankful."

COLOSSIANS 3:15, NIV

MEDITATION

1. Take 30 seconds to sit in silence. Ask God to clear your mind of any distractions.
2. Quietly say, "The peace of Christ is with me."
3. Take a deep breath, letting Christ give you peace.
4. Close your eyes and invite Jesus to be in this moment with you, picturing Him beside you.
5. Look over at Him and thank Him for all He has done for you.
6. Picture Jesus reaching His hand out to you asking you to give Him the worries, fears, and dreams that are occupying your heart.
7. Thinking of each one, place them in His hands, let go, and receive His perfect peace.

30
MARCH

Dear God, today I choose to let go of _____ in my life, and I desire to live in your perfect peace.

31
MARCH

END OF THE MONTH PRACTICE

Positive Thoughts. It's easy to get our minds wrapped up in our troubles and storms. Today, be more aware of the thoughts that come into your mind. If you find they are focused on the waves, tell Jesus you want to fix your eyes on Him instead. Try to catch as many negative thoughts today as you can and replace them with the truth that God is with you, loves you, and can calm this storm, too.

APRIL

PATIENCE

1

"Being strengthened with all power according to his glorious might so that you may have great endurance and patience, and giving joyful thanks to the Father, who has qualified you to share in the inheritance of his holy people in the kingdom of light."

COLOSSIANS 1:11–12, NIV

MEDITATION

1. Sit peacefully in a quiet place.
2. Make your hands into fists and place them on your knees.
3. Say to yourself, "Strengthen me, Lord, with endurance and patience."
4. Receive the Lord's strength in this moment.
5. As you pray, begin to move your left hand toward your left shoulder, as if you are lifting a weight.
6. Do the same with your right hand, feeling God's strength filling you.
7. Pray again: "Strengthen me, Lord, with endurance and patience."

2
APRIL

"The Lord is good to those whose hope is in him,
to the one who seeks him; it is good to wait quietly
for the salvation of the Lord."

LAMENTATIONS 3:25–26, NIV

AFFIRMATION

When I patiently wait on God,
He will be good to me.

3
APRIL

PRAYER PROMPT

God, teach me to patiently wait for you. Help me place my hope
only in your salvation.

4

APRIL

"Through patience a ruler can be persuaded,
and a gentle tongue can break a bone."

PROVERBS 25:15, NIV

MEDITATION

1. Sit in a quiet place away from distractions.
2. Close your eyes and ask God to reveal any political, social, or work-related leaders that have been stressing you out lately.
3. Picture them in God's hands, as His children: beloved, adored, and cherished.
4. Take a few deep breaths, allowing God's peace to pour over you like rain.
5. With a renewed perspective, pray the above verse, Proverbs 25:15.
6. Rest in the knowledge that with patience, even those in authority can be persuaded.
7. Ask God to give you patience and assurance, knowing He is the King of all Kings.

5

"Even youths grow tired and weary, and young men stumble and fall; but those who hope in the Lord will renew their strength."

ISAIAH 40:30–31, NIV

AFFIRMATION

Even when I am tired and weary, God can give me strength.

6

PRAYER PROMPT

Lord, give our leaders patience and strength today in governing our country.

7

"A person's wisdom yields patience; it is to one's glory to overlook an offense."

PROVERBS 19:11, NIV

MEDITATION

1. Find a quiet spot, place a pillow on the floor, and kneel on the pillow.
2. Place your hands to your sides with your palms up.
3. Bask in the ambiance of God's infinite wisdom.
4. Slow your breathing, and quietly repeat, "God, help me be patient."
5. Ask God to reveal any areas of offense in your life.
6. They might be something someone said or did to you, or maybe said or did to others.
7. As you extend your hands in front of you, surrender this offense to God.
8. Ask Him to take this burden from you and replace it with His wisdom and grace.
9. Slowly pull in your hands to your heart while silently saying, "Wisdom yields patience."

8

APRIL

"I remain confident of this: I will see the goodness of
the Lord in the land of the living. Wait for the Lord;
be strong and take heart and wait for the Lord."

PSALM 27:13–14, NIV

AFFIRMATION

*If I remain patient and trust God,
I will see His goodness in my life
and the lives of others.*

9

APRIL

PRAYER PROMPT

I pray for those around the world who are facing trials. Lord,
encourage them today and give them patience to endure in you.

10
APRIL

"Be patient, then, brothers and sisters, until
the Lord's coming. See how the farmer waits for
the land to yield its valuable crop, patiently waiting
for the autumn and spring rains."

JAMES 5:7, NIV

MEDITATION

1. Close your eyes and picture yourself in a field of wheat that is full and ready for harvest.
2. Bask in the rays of the sun shining through the golden brilliance of this essential crop.
3. Admit to God where you are impatient in your life right now.
4. Present your dreams, wishes, and future to Him, knowing He is your good Father.
5. Open your eyes and imagine yourself in that wheat field, aware that God has you right where He wants you during this season of life, knowing the harvest is soon.

11

APRIL

"Be still before the Lord and wait patiently for him;
do not fret when people succeed in their ways,
when they carry out their wicked schemes."

PSALM 37:7, NIV

AFFIRMATION

*I may be surrounded by evil, but
I wait patiently for God's help.*

12

APRIL

PRAYER PROMPT

Lord, encourage people today who are waiting on your provision.
Give them the patience that is only found in you.

13

APRIL

"Brothers and sisters, as an example of patience
in the face of suffering, take the prophets who
spoke in the name of the Lord."

JAMES 5:10, NIV

MEDITATION

1. Find a quiet and safe place in your home where you can sit peacefully.
2. Find your Bible, turn to Genesis 37–50, and reflect on the story of Joseph, who waited 30 years for God's blessing.
3. As you read, take time to picture Joseph in each season of His life, whether in a pit, in prison, or in the throne room waiting with patient endurance for God to bring His promise.
4. Close your eyes and ask God to give you the patient endurance of Joseph.
5. Rest in His perfect peace, receiving the patience that comes with knowing God is in control.

14
APRIL

"And we urge you, brothers and sisters, warn those
who are idle and disruptive, encourage the disheartened,
help the weak, be patient with everyone."

1 THESSALONIANS 5:14, NIV

AFFIRMATION

*When faced with stressful and demanding
situations, I choose to be patient.*

15
APRIL

PRAYER PROMPT

Lord, help people who are working in service industries. Give
them the patience to endure difficult people and give them your
grace to persevere.

16
APRIL

"Let us not become weary in doing good, for at the proper time we will reap a harvest if we do not give up."

GALATIANS 6:9, NIV

MEDITATION

1. Take a deep breath in and do a quick scan of your body, beginning at your fingertips.
2. Where do you feel tired, tense, or overextended?
3. As you breathe out, ask God to use each part of you for good.
4. Hear God tell you to keep pressing on to do good for others in your life.
5. Repeat the phrase: "I will do good for those in need today, God will restore me, and I won't give up."
6. Hear Jesus tell you: "I see the good works of your hands, and will honor you in ways you haven't yet seen."
7. Feel His refreshing truth wash over you in restoration.

17

"For in this hope we were saved. But hope that is seen is no hope at all. Who hopes for what they already have? But if we hope for what we do not yet have, we wait for it patiently."

ROMANS 8:24–25, NIV

AFFIRMATION

I have the patient hope of heaven with Jesus as my Savior, and I can share it with others.

18
APRIL

PRAYER PROMPT

Heavenly Father, you've created me to do good works and help others in need. Help me do your work and wait patiently for your reward.

19

"Rejoice in hope; be patient in affliction; be persistent in prayer."

ROMANS 12:12, NIV

MEDITATION

1. Picture the most peaceful setting imaginable.
2. Now allow Jesus to enter the scene.
3. How does He greet you?
4. Tell Him about something in the world or in your personal life that has been troubling you lately.
5. Hear Him tell you: "I hear you when you pray about this, sweet child; I'm working in wonderful ways."
6. Feel Him exchange these worries with the patient endurance of hope He's building in you.
7. Hear Him say, "Stay connected to me, and I will give you patience despite the circumstance."

20
APRIL

"When the people saw that Moses was so long in coming down from the mountain, they gathered around Aaron and said, 'Come, make us gods who will go before us. As for this fellow Moses who brought us up out of Egypt, we don't know what has happened to him.'"

EXODUS 32:1, NIV

AFFIRMATION

Throughout history, people have been impatient. But I know God is working behind the scenes; I will trust in His timing.

21
APRIL

I pray that my patience can be an example to _____, that they see putting trust in You sets us free.

22
APRIL

Mighty Counselor, you are patient with me when I pour out my heart to you. When I'm tempted, give me a picture of your grace with me.

23

APRIL

"Be still before the Lord and wait patiently for him;
do not fret when people succeed in their ways, when
they carry out their wicked schemes."

PSALM 37:7, NIV

AFFIRMATION

*I trust that God will do everything
He said He will do.*

24

APRIL

PRAYER PROMPT

_____ (a person or situation) has been on my heart lately.
I give them/it to You and ask You to strengthen us in the waiting.

25

"I waited patiently for the Lord; he turned to me
and heard my cry. He lifted me out of the slimy pit,
out of the mud and mire; he set my feet on a rock
and gave me a firm place to stand."

PSALM 40:1–2, NIV

MEDITATION

1. Open your arms in a big stretch and search your heart for what has been troubling you or someone you care about.
2. Cry out to the Lord in prayer.
3. Picture His face turning toward you and hear Him say, "I hear your cry. Whatever you are feeling stuck in, I'm getting you out. Cling to me, the rock that is always unshakable."
4. Wrap your arms around yourself in a hug.
5. Say the words: "I wait patiently for you, Lord and promise keeper."

26
APRIL

"My dear brothers and sisters, take note of this:
Everyone should be quick to listen, slow to speak and
slow to become angry, because human anger does
not produce the righteousness that God desires."

JAMES 1:19–20, NIV

AFFIRMATION

*Because of the patience you show me, I can
be patient with my neighbors, colleagues,
friends, and family members today.*

27
APRIL

"The Lord is not slow in keeping his promise,
as some understand slowness. Instead, he is patient
with you, not wanting anyone to perish, but
everyone to come to repentance."

2 PETER 3:9, NIV

MEDITATION

1. Place your hands over your heart and feel the gentle beating as you take a few deep breaths.
2. Give Jesus a people group or an area of the world that has been troubling your heart or testing your patience recently.
3. Repeat the verse above slowly, each time letting it sink in.
4. Thank God for the times He's been so patient with you.
5. With each inhale, say to yourself, "I trust in Your timing, Lord."
6. With each exhale, say to yourself, "I release my expectations to you, Father."

28

"As you know, we count as blessed those who have persevered. You
have heard of Job's perseverance
and have seen what the Lord finally brought about.
The Lord is full of compassion and mercy."

JAMES 5:11, NIV

MEDITATION

1. Papa God wants to meet you today.
2. Imagine each and every hardship you or someone you know is facing.
3. Drop every negative or worrisome thought into the basket He's holding.
4. Hear God tell you: "I'm with you in these challenges; I see you, I see them."
5. Thank God by saying, "You're full of compassion and mercy. What You will bring about will be better than I could imagine."

29

APRIL

"But do not forget this one thing, dear friends:
With the Lord a day is like a thousand years, and
a thousand years are like a day."

2 PETER 3:8, NIV

AFFIRMATION

*God works outside my concept of time.
I trust Him in all situations, knowing
His timing is perfect.*

30
APRIL

END OF THE MONTH PRACTICE

Doing Good in the Waiting. There are always short and long times of waiting in our lives. Today, each time you encounter a time of waiting, get creative in love. For example, if you are waiting in line at the post office, send a friend an encouraging text, or start a kind conversation with a stranger. As you wait in traffic, pick three cars of people to pray over. The point is to take times that could be annoyances and make them times of blessings for others around you.

MAY

KINDNESS

1

PRAYER PROMPT

Dear Jesus, you've shown me kindness by/when ....
Please help me show kindness to my family, friends, neighbors,
and colleagues today.

2

MAY

"Though the Lord is exalted, he looks kindly on the lowly"

PSALM 138:6, NIV

AFFIRMATION

*I don't need a fancy job title or status
symbols for God to treat me kindly; to Him
I am a VIP no matter where I am in life!*

3

"But when the kindness and love of God our Savior appeared,
he saved us, not because of righteous things we had done, but
because of his mercy. He saved us through the washing of rebirth
and renewal by the Holy Spirit, whom he poured out on us
generously through Jesus Christ our Savior, so that, having been
justified by his grace, we might become heirs having
the hope of eternal life."

TITUS 3:4–7, NIV

MEDITATION

1. As you reread the scripture above several times, think about God's
   kindness to you.
2. As you breathe in, repeat to yourself, "Jesus saves me."
3. As you breathe out, repeat to yourself, "Not with my own strength, but
   His mercy."
4. Picture Jesus's loving kindness pouring over your heart, filling up your soul.

4
MAY

Holy Spirit, I saw your beautiful kindness today through ....
(a person, situation, etc.), and I thank you.

5
MAY

My Savior and Redeemer, help me show extra compassion to
.... today. I need your help. Thanks for your great
kindness to me, a perfect model of how I should be.

6

"But love your enemies, do good to them, and lend to them without expecting to get anything back. Then your reward
will be great, and you will be children of the Most High, because he is kind to the ungrateful and wicked."

LUKE 6:35, NIV

MEDITATION

1. Picture Jesus sitting next to you right now as you take a few deep breaths.
2. Feel Him calming your heart and mind.
3. He loves these special meetings with you.
4. He hates when anyone hurts you. He is your guardian.
5. Hear Him whisper to you, "I've forgiven you, so you can forgive those who hurt you."
6. Say to Him, "You're my defender, you're the judge; now I get to forgive and love."
7. Feel His kindness, peace, and forgiveness infuse your heart.

7
MAY

"Be devoted to one another in love. Honor
one another above yourselves."

ROMANS 12:10, NIV

AFFIRMATION

*You honor me above yourself, Jesus. Help me
follow in your footsteps and extend a
bouquet of kindness to each person I see
in front of me, both in person and online today.*

8

"Whoever is kind to the poor lends to the Lord, and
he will reward them for what they have done."

PROVERBS 19:17, NIV

AFFIRMATION

*As I show kindness to others, I won't seek
praise or thanks from others. I know my
reward is in heaven.*

9
MAY

"Do not forget to show hospitality to strangers,
for by so doing some people have shown hospitality
to angels without knowing it."

HEBREWS 13:2, NIV

MEDITATION

1. Look around you as you take a few deep breaths.
2. Thank God for something you can see, something you can taste, something you can smell, something you can touch, and something you can hear.
3. Tell God the ways He's showing you love through these things.
4. Now imagine things that your senses might not pick up on, such as love, angels, protection, etc.
5. Thank Him for showering you with all those kindnesses.
6. Ask Jesus if there's any way you can share His love with acts of hospitality today.
7. If you don't hear an immediate response, look for His answer throughout your day.

10
MAY

Everlasting Father, please enable me to be a blessing to someone who might feel left out this week.

11
MAY

"You, my brothers and sisters, were called to be free. But do not use your freedom to indulge the flesh; rather, serve one another humbly in love."

GALATIANS 5:13, NIV

AFFIRMATION

You are King of Kings yet came to be a servant of all. I will follow your example today.

12
MAY

"And God raised us up with Christ and seated us with him in the heavenly realms in Christ Jesus, in order that in the coming ages he might show the incomparable riches of his grace, expressed in his kindness to us in Christ Jesus."

EPHESIANS 2:6–7, NIV

MEDITATION

1. Take a pause from the outside world as you picture placing your burdens into Jesus's hands.
2. Read the verse above slowly, letting the Holy Spirit highlight whatever He needs you to hear.
3. What words stick out to you?
4. Repeat them again as you feel His truth sink deep into your heart.
5. Breathe in the truth and say to yourself, "God raised us up with Christ."
6. Exhale your worries.
7. Reflect on "the incomparable riches of His grace, expressed in His kindness to you in Christ Jesus."

13
MAY

Mighty Counselor, please heal my heart from unkindness done to me and my loved ones. Please fill me up once again with your loving kindness.

14
MAY

"Do to others as you would have them do to you."

LUKE 6:31, NIV

AFFIRMATION

I will treat others the way I want to be treated today. I'll show compassion to them through my thoughts and actions.

103

15

MAY

"In everything I did, I showed you that by this kind
of hard work we must help the weak, remembering
the words the Lord Jesus himself said: 'It is more
blessed to give than to receive.'"

ACTS 20:35, NIV

MEDITATION

1. Stretch your arms up into the sky and take a deep breath.
2. Feel your body relax and let go of any tension you feel as you bring your arms to your side.
3. Inhale while saying to yourself, "I am more blessed to give."
4. Exhale while saying to yourself, "Than to receive."
5. Then, as you breathe in, say to yourself, "Because Jesus fills me up with His strength."
6. And as you breathe out, say to yourself, "I can help those around me today."
7. Picture God's loving kindness filling you up.
8. Feel the strength to help others.

16
MAY

God my Redeemer, please help my heart and words reflect your kindness today.

17
MAY

"You gave me life and showed me kindness, and in your providence watched over my spirit."

JOB 10:12, NIV

AFFIRMATION

Because of my love for Jesus, I will care for others with kindness today, looking out for their best interest.

18
MAY

"Dear children, let us not love with words or speech
but with actions and in truth."

1 JOHN 3:18, NIV

MEDITATION

1. Go to your quiet place.
2. Slow your breathing by taking long deep breaths.
3. Ask God to bring someone to mind who did something out of the ordinary to be kind to you.
4. Meditate on why this made an impression on you.
5. Think of one action you can take to be kind to a friend, family member, or stranger today.
6. With each inhale, think: "Not with words or speech."
7. With each exhale, think: "But with actions and truth."
8. Set out to show love and kindness to one person today with your actions and truth.

19
MAY

Today, I lift up _____, who has been kind to me lately. I pray that they will experience extraordinary kindness from others this week.

20
MAY

"It is a sin to despise one's neighbor, but blessed
is the one who is kind to the needy."

PROVERBS 14:21, NIV

AFFIRMATION

*It is a blessing to treat those in need
with kindness, gentleness, and honor.*

21
MAY

"The foreigner residing among you must be treated as your native-born. Love them as yourself, for you were foreigners in Egypt. I am the Lord your God."

LEVITICUS 19:34, NIV

MEDITATION

1. Close your eyes and sit in peaceful silence.
2. Meditate on how you feel at home in your own space.
3. Switch your focus to a moment where you felt out of place.
4. Think about what it felt like: How was it difficult for you?
5. Picture those who are feeling scared, lost, or unwelcomed.
6. See them as God's children, beloved and created with purpose.
7. Pray silently: "Lord, I place those who are in a foreign land into your hands. Allow me to be kind to them when they cross my path."

22
MAY

PRAYER PROMPT

Pray for a goal you want to accomplish. Ask for God to help you achieve it with His kindness and grace.

23
MAY

"The hearts of the wise make their mouths prudent, and their lips promote instruction. Gracious words are a honeycomb, sweet to the soul and healing to the bones."

PROVERBS 16:23–24, NIV

AFFIRMATION

I will receive kind words spoken to me, deep in my heart, and allow them to encourage me.

24
MAY

"Anxiety weighs down the heart, but a kind word cheers it up."

PROVERBS 12:25, NIV

MEDITATION

1. Find a quiet place and get comfortable.
2. Relax your body; release any tension or burdens you are carrying.
3. Close your eyes and picture Jesus standing in front of you.
4. Look into His eyes; see that He is so happy to be here with you at this moment.
5. Receive these words from Him: "I love you beyond measure."
6. Bask in these words.
7. Receive the kindness of His voice.
8. As you go about the rest of your day, let this interaction with Jesus encourage and uplift your spirit.

25
MAY

Pray for people to be kind to one another when posting online. Pray that God will help people think before they type.

26
MAY

"The islanders showed us unusual kindness. They built a fire and welcomed us all because it was raining and cold."

ACTS 28:2, NIV

AFFIRMATION

Extra kindness makes a stranger feel at home; I choose to be kind to those I meet today.

27
MAY

"Therefore, as God's chosen people, holy and dearly loved, clothe yourselves with compassion, kindness, humility, gentleness and patience."

COLOSSIANS 3:12, NIV

MEDITATION

1. Find a place to stand in peaceful surrender.
2. Say to yourself, "I am chosen by God."
3. Imagine holding a shirt, full of compassion. Pretend to put that shirt on and let compassion flow into your heart.
4. In the same way, imagine pants, full of kindness. Put on those pants, allowing kindness to flow throughout your body.
5. Do the same for a hat of gentleness and shoes of patience.
6. Allow these attributes to permeate your very being today, being clothed as God's chosen.

28
MAY

Heavenly Father, help me refrain from speaking poorly of others, and let only kindness come from my mouth today.

29
MAY

"'But let the one who boasts boast about this: that they have the understanding to know me, that I am the Lord, who exercises kindness, justice and righteousness on earth, for in these I delight,' declares the Lord."

JEREMIAH 9:24, NIV

AFFIRMATION

Today, I choose to show kindness, justice, and righteousness in my actions.

30
MAY

Sometimes it's hard to accept help. God, help me receive other people's kindnesses gracefully.

31
MAY

Old-Fashioned Kindness. Think of someone who recently showed kindness to you. By hand, write them a letter explaining why their kindness meant so much, and how thankful you are for what they did. Place the letter in an envelope and deliver it to them. Showing appreciation for others helps the initial act of kindness continue. Taking the time to write a letter is a special touch that is especially appreciated these days.

JUNE

FORGIVENESS

1

JUNE

Jesus, knowing we don't have to forgive out of our own strength, but rather out of reverence for what you did on the cross, makes it much easier. Thank you.

2
JUNE

"The Lord is slow to anger but great in power;
the Lord will not leave the guilty unpunished."

NAHUM 1:3, NIV

AFFIRMATION

*Anger in and of itself is not a sin. God cares
about our pain and wants us to let
Him be our redeemer and healer.*

3
JUNE

PRAYER PROMPT

Pray for someone from whom you have received forgiveness.
Pray that God will give them peace and blessings today.

4

"If we confess our sins, he is faithful and just and will forgive us our sins and purify us from all unrighteousness."

1 JOHN 1:9, NIV

MEDITATION

1. Go to your safe place and rest in peaceful silence.
2. Close your eyes. Place your arms at your sides with your palms facing up.
3. Ask God to reveal any areas in your life that you need to confess to Him.
4. Pray silently: "Father, you are faithful and just. Please forgive me for _____."
5. Confess to Him what is in your heart, placing any past or present sins into His forgiving hands.
6. With each confession, allow His love to wash you clean.
7. Once you finish, recite and receive the power of these words: "By the blood of Jesus, I am forgiven."

5

"For our struggle is not against flesh and blood, but ... against the spiritual forces of evil in the heavenly realms."

EPHESIANS 6:12, NIV

AFFIRMATION

My battle isn't really against (a person), but rather it's against the evil that's corrupting others and causing division. The enemy wants us to be divided; Jesus wants us to forgive others so we can be unified.

6
JUNE

"You, Lord, are forgiving and good, abounding in love to all who call to you."

PSALM 86:5, NIV

MEDITATION

1. Find a quiet place where you can get on your knees in reverence to God.
2. Take a few deep breaths and allow His goodness to surround you.
3. Imagine a child with their father.
4. See how the father delights when the child says, "Daddy, I love you."
5. Even when the child does something wrong, the father embraces and delights in the child.
6. Make a special note of how the father smiles at the child.
7. In the same way, God delights in you.
8. Picture God smiling at you as you say, "Father, I love you."
9. Let the warmth of His forgiveness and love fill your heart.

7
JUNE

Thank you, Jesus, for taking the death penalty meant for me. When I experience someone hurting, help me say I'm sorry, even if I'm unrelated to their pain.

8
JUNE

"Having canceled the charge of our legal indebtedness, which stood against us and condemned us; he has taken it away, nailing it to the cross."

COLOSSIANS 2:14, NIV

AFFIRMATION

Jesus loves me so much that He canceled the debt for my sins.

9
JUNE

"Be kind and compassionate to one another, forgiving each other, just as in Christ God forgave you."

EPHESIANS 4:32, NIV

MEDITATION

1. Find a place to sit peacefully.
2. Close your eyes and ask God to bring one person to mind who you have had trouble forgiving lately.
3. Say to yourself, "Jesus, you forgave me even when I didn't deserve it."
4. Take a deep breath and say, "Help me forgive this person in the same way."
5. Picture Jesus nodding and placing His hands on your shoulders. Take another deep breath and say, "Father, take this burden from me, and help me move forward in your peace."
6. Feel His peace flowing through you.

10
JUNE

God, I release _____ (a person) to you. I don't want to be their judge; I ask for your forgiveness in judging them.

11
JUNE

"Do not judge, and you will not be judged. Do not condemn, and you will not be condemned. Forgive, and you will be forgiven."

LUKE 6:37, NIV

AFFIRMATION

God is the judge; this allows me to forgive others and choose compassion.

12
JUNE

"And when you stand praying, if you hold anything
against anyone, forgive them, so that your Father
in heaven may forgive you your sins."

MARK 11:25, NIV

MEDITATION

1. Find a peaceful place to stand.
2. Take a deep breath and say to yourself, "Father, as I choose to forgive others, please forgive me."
3. Picture someone toward whom you have recently held judgment.
4. Ask God for forgiveness in holding judgment.
5. Quietly recite the following: "God, you are the judge and I am not. Help me release other people's actions to you. Today, I choose to love others the way you love me."
6. Feel the weight of judgment fall off your shoulders.
7. Now that you are free of this burden, choose to walk today in love, joy, and peace.

13

"Bear with each other and forgive one another
if any of you has a grievance against someone.
Forgive as the Lord forgave you."

COLOSSIANS 3:13, NIV

AFFIRMATION

*God forgave me, so now I choose
to forgive those who have wronged me.
It doesn't mean I excuse or accept their
behavior. But I release the pain to God and
thank Him for His goodness.*

14
JUNE

Father, you command me to forgive; you don't command a close relationship. Please give me wisdom and help me set good boundaries.

15
JUNE

"Therefore, confess your sins to each other and pray for each other so that you may be healed. The prayer of a righteous person is powerful and effective."

JAMES 5:16, NIV

AFFIRMATION

Persistence in prayer gives me the strength to forgive and love others.

16
JUNE

Jesus, help me not judge other people's sins but look at my friends, family, neighbors, and people online with love, grace, and forgiveness.

17
JUNE

"For all have sinned and fall short of the glory of God."

ROMANS 3:23, NIV

AFFIRMATION

Jesus died for all of us, He sets us free to see ourselves and others through His lens of love.

18
JUNE

"Make sure that nobody pays back wrong for wrong,
but always strive to do what is good for each other
and for everyone else."

1 THESSALONIANS 5:15, NIV

MEDITATION

1. Place your hands on your knees with your palms facing down.
2. As you take a deep breath, release to Jesus any wrong done to you or some-one you care about.
3. As you surrender, repeat to yourself, "I will not pay back wrong for wrong."
4. Now flip your hands up as you imagine God's goodness filling you with His love.
5. Picture Him saying, "I've forgiven you. I will now help you do good for those who have hurt you."
6. Silently commit to do good to those around you today.

19
JUNE

PRAYER PROMPT

Please help me hold on to your truth in my actions and thoughts
today and let go of any grudges I may be carrying.

20
JUNE

"To the praise of his glorious grace, which he has
freely given us in the One he loves. In him we have redemption
through his blood, the forgiveness of sins,
in accordance with the riches of God's grace."

EPHESIANS 1:6–7, NIV

AFFIRMATION

*I am fully redeemed because of the blood of
Jesus. I will act in full appreciation today.*

21
JUNE

"Then Peter came to Jesus and asked, 'Lord, how many times shall I forgive my brother or sister who sins against me?
Up to seven times?' Jesus answered, 'I tell you, not seven times, but seventy-seven times.'"

MATTHEW 18:21–22, NIV

MEDITATION

1. Picture yourself sitting with Jesus and His disciples the day Peter asked Jesus this question.
2. As you breathe in, quietly ask Jesus, "How many times should I forgive _____ (a person)?"
3. As you breathe out, picture Jesus saying, "As many times as you've been hurt or offended."
4. Meditate on that concept.
5. As you keep taking deep breaths, allow God's forgiveness of *you* to fill your soul. After all, He has forgiven you as many times as you've offended.
6. Quietly say, "Out of His overflow of love and forgiveness for me, I'm enabled to love and forgive those who have hurt me."

22
JUNE

Dear God, as I pray for _____ who has hurt me in the past, please trade the pain in my heart for love.

23
JUNE

"But if you do not forgive others their sins, your Father will not forgive your sins."

MATTHEW 6:15, NIV

AFFIRMATION

As I choose forgiveness, it's like being freed from a prison cell and realizing I held the key the whole time.

24
JUNE

"He does not treat us as our sins deserve or repay
us according to our iniquities. For as high as the heavens
are above the earth, so great is his love for those
who fear him; as far as the east is from the west, so far
has he removed our transgressions from us."

PSALM 103:10–12, NIV

MEDITATION

1. Stretch out your arms as far apart as possible.
2. Picture two strings, one tied to each hand, going as far into the universe as possible in either direction.
3. The strings don't touch but continue forever.
4. Now picture Jesus's eyes of love looking at you as He says, "I've removed your past mistakes farther than these strings are away from you."
5. Look at your hands and picture how Jesus's hands were on the cross.
6. Say to yourself, "That's how much He loves me; that's how much I'm forgiven."

25

PRAYER PROMPT

Forgiving Father, I pray for those who feel shame today and are overwhelmed by their past mistakes.

26
JUNE

"Hatred stirs up conflict, but love covers over all wrongs."

PROVERBS 10:12, NIV

AFFIRMATION

The shame others caused you is not okay. That's not the way it should be. But each time your pain is triggered and you choose to forgive, you're the one that gets set free.

27
JUNE

"'Come now, let us settle the matter,' says the Lord.
'Though your sins are like scarlet, they shall be
as white as snow; though they are red as crimson,
they shall be like wool.'"

ISAIAH 1:18, NIV

MEDITATION

1. Close your eyes and picture a landscape covered in beautiful freshly fallen snow.
2. Imagine the quiet of the land as you sit with Jesus under a tree.
3. Take a few deep breaths and confess to Him any guilt you're carrying today.
4. Hear Jesus say to you, "Although you've been overwhelmed by your past, I have made you completely clean and new."
5. Picture Jesus making your soul as fresh as that newly fallen snow.
6. Say, "I'm sorry for all I've done, Jesus; thank you for dying for me," and hear Him respond, "I hear you child, you are completely forgiven!"

28
JUNE

PRAYER PROMPT

Pray for forgiveness for a situation that you handled poorly recently. Ask God to cleanse your heart and mind.

29
JUNE

"For he has rescued us from the dominion of darkness and brought us into the kingdom of the Son he loves, in whom we have redemption, the forgiveness of sins."

COLOSSIANS 1:13–14, NIV

AFFIRMATION

I'm no longer judged for my past. I'm brought into Jesus's kingdom as a redeemed child of God!

30

JUNE

END OF THE MONTH PRACTICE

Your Load Can Be Light. Grab a backpack, fill it with rocks until it's heavy, and walk around with it on your back. Feel the weight. Take out one rock at a time, associating it with a bitterness toward another person, yourself, or God. As you let go of the pain, say, "Jesus, I'm sorry; thank you for forgiving me. I choose to forgive .... Help me be filled up with your love." Feel the bitterness lift off your back and your soul with each rock you remove. God doesn't call us to be best friends with everyone, but He does command us to forgive everyone. Continue until all the offenses you can think of are off your back.

JULY

HOPE

1

JULY

PRAYER PROMPT

Dear Jesus, so many people are in desperate need of your hope. Please remind us of all the hope that's in You.

2

JULY

"If you remain in me and my words remain in you, ask whatever you wish, and it will be done for you."

JOHN 15:7, NIV

AFFIRMATION

No matter what I hope for, I trust that God will make it happen.

3

"…We also glory in our sufferings, because we know that suffering produces perseverance; perseverance, character; and character, hope. And hope does not put us to shame, because God's love has been poured out into our hearts through the Holy Spirit, who has been given to us."

ROMANS 5:3–5, NIV

MEDITATION

1. Take a deep breath in and be filled with Holy Spirit's hope as you read the words above.
2. Tell your Heavenly Father some of the ways you've been suffering.
3. Repeat these words: "Suffering produces perseverance; perseverance, character; and character, hope."
4. Hear Jesus tell you: "Hope does not put you to shame. My love is being poured out into your heart."
5. Feel the warmth of His love.

JULY

Jesus, I'm asking for your help to see my current problem with a bigger and better perspective.

JULY

"Now faith is confidence in what we hope for and assurance about what we do not see."

HEBREWS 11:1, NIV

AFFIRMATION

My hope is in Jesus's death and resurrection, which can never be taken away.

6

JULY

"I wait for the Lord, my whole being waits,
and in his word, I put my hope."

PSALM 130:5, NIV

MEDITATION

1. Let your spirit rest in God's presence today.
2. As you take a deep breath in, say to yourself, "I put my hope in God's word."
3. As you breathe out, say to yourself, "My whole being waits for the Lord."
4. Keep repeating these truths as you breathe in and out.
5. Experience the words sinking deeper into your heart and mind with each breath.
6. Be aware of any resistance to these truths.
7. If anything feels blocked, submit it to Jesus.
8. To close the meditation, say, "I have unfailing hope in you!"

7
JULY

Dear Jesus, thanks for caring about all areas of my life. I put my relationships, my work, my health, my everything into Your loving hands today.

8
JULY

"May the God of hope fill you with all joy and peace as you trust in him, so that you may overflow with hope by the power of the Holy Spirit."

ROMANS 15:13, NIV

AFFIRMATION

I will overflow with hope as I trust in Jesus!

9

"... We wait eagerly for our adoption to sonship,
the redemption of our bodies."

ROMANS 8:23, NIV

MEDITATION

1. Close your eyes and picture yourself cradled in God's tender arms.
2. Jesus wants to restore you.
3. What part of your life is particularly tiring these days? Offer it up to God.
4. Hear Jesus say, "I'm renewing you, my sweet child."
5. Respond quietly, "I'm adopted into God's family. I am renewed in the Lord; my hope is in Him."
6. Allow the Holy Spirit to fill you with His presence and renewal.

10
JULY

Dear God, I'm hoping for _____ (a hope, dream, or desire) in my life. Help me surrender this want to you and entrust the hope in this area of my life to you.

11
JULY

"Hope deferred makes the heart sick, but a longing fulfilled is a tree of life."

PROVERBS 13:12, NIV

AFFIRMATION

Jesus fulfills the deepest longing of my soul; therefore, I always have hope.

12
JULY

"If only for this life we have hope in Christ, we are of all people most to be pitied. But Christ has indeed been raised from the dead, the first fruits of those who have fallen asleep."

1 CORINTHIANS 15:19–20, NIV

MEDITATION

1. Be still and know that God is with you.
2. As you take a deep breath in, say to yourself, "Jesus has conquered death."
3. As you exhale, say to yourself, "My hope is in the risen Christ."
4. As you let your whole body relax, picture Jesus in all His glory on the throne in heaven.
5. Hear Him say, "I'm giving you the hope of eternal life!"
6. Picture heaven, with no more pain, suffering, or tears.
7. Let this hope fill every ounce of your being.

13
JULY

Holy Spirit, I pray for those who are being persecuted for their faith in you. Please renew them with your hope today!

14
JULY

"To them God has chosen to make known among the Gentiles the glorious riches of this mystery, which is Christ in you, the hope of glory."

COLOSSIANS 1:27, NIV

AFFIRMATION

I will share Jesus's love with those who don't know His hope. His glory is in me!

15

JULY

"But those who hope in the Lord will renew their strength. They will soar on wings like eagles; they will run and not grow weary; they will walk and not be faint."

ISAIAH 40:31, NIV

MEDITATION

1. Imagine taking God's hand, and picture Him leading you down a beautiful pathway.
2. Tell Jesus what's been weighing down your heart recently.
3. He wants to lift those burdens from your soul.
4. Imagine you're now soaring in the sky with Jesus.
5. Hear Him say, "I'm taking care of all the things you worry about."
6. Tell Him: "My hope is in you, Lord. I trust you with it all."

16
JULY

Pray for those less fortunate than you, that Jesus would comfort them today and fill them with hope for the future.

17
JULY

"Praise be to the God and Father of our Lord Jesus Christ! In his great mercy he has given us new birth into a living hope through the resurrection of Jesus Christ from the dead."

1 PETER 1:3, NIV

AFFIRMATION

Through Jesus, I have a living hope.

18
JULY

"Rejoice in the Lord and be glad, you righteous;
sing, all you who are upright in heart!"

PSALM 32:11, NIV

MEDITATION

1. Sitting in stillness, let God's hope bring you joy in this moment.
2. Get on your knees and bring your hands to prayer.
3. Repeat to yourself, "Joyful in hope, patient in affliction, faithful in prayer."
4. Take time to notice Him right beside you, guiding you, protecting you, and loving you.
5. Let the knowledge of His presence bring you hope.
6. Finish by praying: "Father, because of your presence in my life, I can have hope in you alone."

19
JULY

Jesus, I feel so hopeless because of _____ (a situation) in my life. Strengthen me today with the hope of salvation found only in you.

20
JULY

"I pray that the eyes of your heart may be enlightened in order that you may know the hope to which he has called you, the riches of his glorious inheritance in his holy people."

EPHESIANS 1:18, NIV

AFFIRMATION

My heart is full of hope because I know Jesus has so much in store for me.

21

"You are my refuge and my shield; I have put my hope in your word."

PSALM 119:114, NIV

MEDITATION

1. Close your eyes and picture a battlefield filled with knights.
2. See yourself on the field as you prepare for battle by putting on armor and grabbing a shield.
3. Imagine the shield is extremely thick. Nothing can pierce through it. Notice as you pick it up, though, that it is as light as a feather.
4. As you look up, you see God the Father. He says to you, "I am your refuge and your shield. You can place your hope in me."
5. Knowing that an impenetrable shield is in your life in the form of God, walk with confident hope today that He will protect you from any opposition you face.

22
JULY

Holy Spirit, help me inspire others to have hope in whatever circumstances they face in their lives.

23
JULY

"We remember before our God and Father your work produced by faith, your labor prompted by love, and your endurance inspired by hope in our Lord Jesus Christ."

1 THESSALONIANS 1:3, NIV

AFFIRMATION

God gives me the strength to have faith, hope, and love in my life.

24
JULY

"But as for me, I watch in hope for the Lord,
I wait for God my Savior; my God will hear me."

MICAH 7:7, NIV

MEDITATION

1. Take a few deep breaths.
2. With each inhale, say to yourself, "I watch in hope for the Lord."
3. With each exhale, say to yourself, "I wait for God my Savior."
4. Placing your hands on your sides, feel the worries from your day run off your shoulders and drip off your hands like water.
5. Notice you begin to feel light, fresh, and clean, as if you've just had a shower.
6. Silently pray: "God, I know you listen to me; fill me today with hope."
7. Pay close attention to your senses and feel Him filling you from your toes to your head with His holy, lovely, and joyful hope.

25
JULY

PRAYER PROMPT

Jesus, thank you for redeeming me from my past. Your love for me gives me hope for the future.

26
JULY

"Let us hold unswervingly to the hope we profess,
for he who promised is faithful."

HEBREWS 10:23, NIV

AFFIRMATION

*God is faithful in all circumstances; therefore,
I can have hope in all circumstances.*

27
JULY

"Oh, that I might have my request, that God would grant what I hope for"

JOB 6:8, NIV

MEDITATION

1. Think carefully about an area in your life in which you feel hopeless.
2. Notice your feelings, emotions, and worries about it.
3. Close your eyes, and picture Jesus standing in front of you.
4. Tell Him in detail why you feel hopeless.
5. Hear Him say, "I am so sorry you feel hopeless. You don't have to anymore. I am here, and I can make all things new."
6. Allow those words to sink in; feel the warmth of His love cause the hopelessness to dissolve and allow new hope to form.
7. Picture Jesus reaching His arms out to hug you. Receive His embrace.

28
JULY

PRAYER PROMPT

Pray for a friend or family member who is facing a difficult situation and feels hopeless.

29
JULY

"There is surely a future hope for you, and your hope will not be cut off."

PROVERBS 23:18, NIV

AFFIRMATION

At all times, God is working things out for the best for me.

30
JULY

PRAYER PROMPT

Pray for those who have lost their homes or jobs during a difficult season, that God will restore their hope, and bring new blessings in their lives.

31
JULY

END OF THE MONTH PRACTICE

Bible Verse Giveaway Challenge. This world is in desperate need of hope! People put their hope in so many things that eventually let them down. Jesus is the only answer to unshakable hope. Be a hope bringer this week! Pick several verses from the past month and print, write, or type them out. You can get creative if you'd like or keep it simple. Then give them away! Hand them (or send them) to strangers, friends, family, people online, colleagues, and neighbors. Hearing God's word on hope could change those people's lives forever!

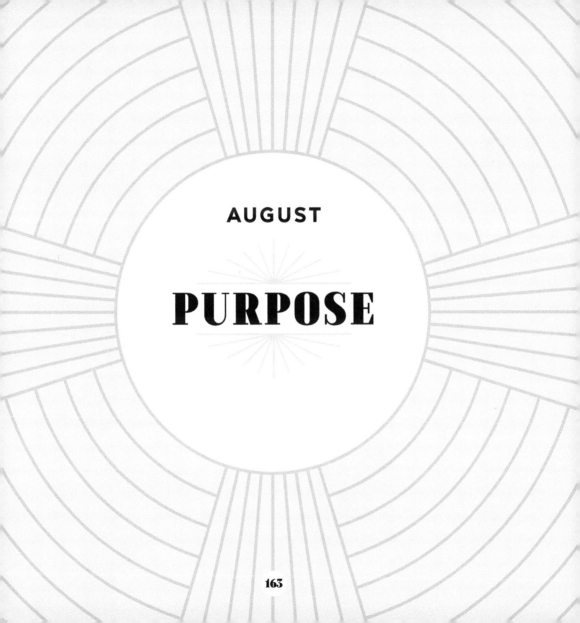

AUGUST

PURPOSE

1

AUGUST

PRAYER PROMPT

God of Heaven's Armies, remind me and my loved ones of our purpose in you!

2

AUGUST

"'For I know the plans I have for you,' declares the Lord,
'plans to prosper you and not to harm you, plans
to give you hope and a future.'"

JEREMIAH 29:11, NIV

AFFIRMATION

God has great plans for me, and my
future is filled with purpose!

3

"You are the salt of the earth. But if the salt loses its saltiness, how can it be made salty again? It is no longer good for anything, except to be thrown out and trampled underfoot. You are the light of the world. A town built on a hill cannot be hidden. Neither do people light a lamp and put it under a bowl. Instead, they put it on its stand, and it gives light to everyone in the house. In the same way, let your light shine before others, that they may see your good deeds and glorify your Father in heaven."

MATTHEW 5:13–16, NIV

MEDITATION

1. Read and reread the scripture above several times slowly, as you take deep breaths.
2. Picture each and every word coming to life.
3. Hear Jesus saying to you, "My light will shine through you as you trust in me."
4. Say out loud, "I am radiant with God's love; I will shine it to the world!"

4
AUGUST

Holy Spirit, please fill me up with your light so I can have purpose in shining your light to others.

5
AUGUST

"But you are a chosen people, a royal priesthood, a holy nation, God's special possession, that you may declare the praises of him who called you out of darkness into his wonderful light."

1 PETER 2:9, NIV

AFFIRMATION

I will share God's light with those around me today!

6

"For in him all things were created: things in heaven
and on earth, visible and invisible, whether thrones
or powers or rulers or authorities; all things have been created
through him and for him."

COLOSSIANS 1:16, NIV

MEDITATION

1. Put your hands over your heart as you slow down to meet with Jesus.
2. Close your eyes and picture complete and total darkness all over
   the universe.
3. Now picture God saying a word and creating the world.
4. That same God who created heaven and earth chose you.
5. Meditate on the purpose that comes with that fact, and on these words:
   "I created you for a purpose. I have good plans for your life."

7

AUGUST

PRAYER PROMPT

God, lead those who feel lost. Help them know you have great plans for their life!

8

AUGUST

"Many are the plans in a person's heart, but it is the Lord's purpose that prevails."

PROVERBS 19:21, NIV

AFFIRMATION

I will put my trust in God, and His purpose for my life will prevail and never fail.

9

"Then Jesus came to them and said, 'All authority in heaven and on earth has been given to me. Therefore go and make disciples of all nations, baptizing them in the name of the Father and of the Son and of the Holy Spirit, and teaching them to obey everything I have commanded you. And surely I am with you always, to the very end of the age.'"

MATTHEW 28:18–20, NIV

MEDITATION

1. Imagine a peaceful place to sit with Jesus and feel His presence.
2. Hear Him say, "Go and make disciples of all nations, I will be with you always, child. I will never leave you."
3. Ask Jesus to help you tell others about His love. Then say, "Thanks for the purpose you give me!"
4. Sit in stillness for a few more moments, allowing Him to speak to you.

10

PRAYER PROMPT

Jesus, I want my work to have purpose. Lead me to the right job for me and allow me to work my current job out of love for you.

11

AUGUST

"For we are God's handiwork, created in Christ Jesus to do good works, which God prepared in advance for us to do."

EPHESIANS 2:10, NIV

AFFIRMATION

I'm God's masterpiece, created to do good works and share His love.

12
AUGUST

"…He marked out their appointed times in history and the boundaries of their lands. God did this so that they would seek him and perhaps reach out for him and find him, though he is not far from any one of us. 'For in him we live and move and have our being.' As some of your own poets have said, 'We are his offspring.'"

ACTS 17:26–28, NIV

MEDITATION

1. Picture your life flashing before your eyes like a movie.
2. What moments need healing or purpose?
3. Invite Jesus into each scene.
4. Hear God tell you: "I love you. I've planned you for a good purpose. I created you to know me."
5. Let that truth be etched in every piece of your life story as you reach out to Jesus.

13

AUGUST

I pray for _____ (a country/city in the world) to hear the Gospel, and to know your purpose for the lives of all those living there.

14

AUGUST

"And we know that in all things God works for the good of those who love him, who have been called according to his purpose."

ROMANS 8:28, NIV

AFFIRMATION

No trial can hinder God's purpose for my life as I walk in fellowship with Him!

15

"So, he said to me, 'This is the word of the Lord to
Zerubbabel: "Not by might nor by power, but by
my Spirit",' says the Lord Almighty."

ZECHARIAH 4:6, NIV

MEDITATION

1. Get on your knees and place your hands to your sides with your palms facing up.
2. In peaceful silence, think of something stressful at work you have been dealing with by yourself.
3. Ask for God's help.
4. Silently pray: "Not by my strength, but by your spirit."
5. Picture Him saying, "You don't have to do this alone. By my spirit, I can take this burden from you."
6. Release this burden and offer it to God.
7. As you go about your workday, know that nothing is too big for you and God to handle together.

16

AUGUST

Pray for children, that God would ignite a fire in their hearts to live a solid life of purpose.

17

AUGUST

"But the plans of the Lord stand firm forever, the purposes of his heart through all generations."

PSALM 33:11, NIV

AFFIRMATION

God's plan for me is strong and firm. I can trust His purpose for my life.

18

*"So whether you eat or drink or whatever you do,
do it all for the glory of God."*

1 CORINTHIANS 10:31, NIV

MEDITATION

1. Find a quiet place to sit.
2. Think of the tasks you must complete today, and all the things you need to do to get them done.
3. Picture God in the room with you, watching you get these tasks done. How would He describe your work ethic and attitude?
4. Reflect on the effort you put into your tasks and ask God if He wants you to do anything differently.
5. Quietly say, "Lord, today I dedicate these things to you. I will work my hardest to do them in a way that honors you."

19

PRAYER PROMPT

Jesus, no matter what hard tasks I must complete at work, help me have the strength to finish them well and honor you in the process.

20

AUGUST

"But seek first his kingdom and his righteousness, and all these things will be given to you as well."

MATTHEW 6:33, NIV

AFFIRMATION

If I seek the Lord first, He will give me the desires of my heart.

21

"There is a time for everything, and a season for
every activity under the heavens."

ECCLESIASTES 3:1, NIV

MEDITATION

1. Find a peaceful space to stand, with your feet shoulder-width apart and your arms at your sides.
2. Ask God to meet you in this moment, and feel His presence around you, filling you with peace.
3. Take a few deep breaths.
4. With each inhale, think: "There is a time for everything."
5. With each exhale, think: "God is with me through it all."
6. Bowing your head in prayer, ask God to reveal what He is teaching you in this specific season of your life.
7. In silence, wait for Him to respond, making note of thoughts and feelings you experience.
8. Close your time by thanking God for one blessing in your life right now.

22
AUGUST

PRAYER PROMPT

Pray for college students, that God would give them direction on the purpose they have for their lives.

23
AUGUST

"I will instruct you and teach you in the way you should go;
I will counsel you with my loving eye on you."

PSALM 32:8, NIV

AFFIRMATION

*If I renew my focus on God,
He will direct my path.*

24

"I know that you can do all things; no purpose of yours can be thwarted."

JOB 42:2, NIV

MEDITATION

1. Rest in peaceful silence and allow the peace of God to cover you like a warm sweater.
2. Take a few slow, deep breaths, each time relaxing your muscles in your body, from your head down to your toes.
3. Picture the dream you have for your life.
4. Describe your dream to God, why you love it, why you want to accomplish it, and how it makes you feel purposeful.
5. Picture His loving expression, hanging on your every word.
6. Listen as He says, "Your dream is important to me. Through me you can accomplish all things."
7. Receive His words of love and walk into your purpose with His strength.

25
AUGUST

PRAYER PROMPT

God, I place my future in your hands, help me believe that you always make good on the promises you speak over me.

26
AUGUST

"Before I formed you in the womb I knew you, before you were born, I set you apart; I appointed you as a prophet to the nations."

JEREMIAH 1:5, NIV

AFFIRMATION

Even before I was born, God knew me and had a purpose for me.

27
AUGUST

"The purposes of a person's heart are deep waters,
but one who has insight draws them out."

PROVERBS 20:5, NIV

MEDITATION

1. Wherever you are, close your eyes and slow your breathing.
2. Ask God to reveal His purpose for you.
3. Allow time to sit in silence. Give God the space to respond.
4. Ask God to show you a picture of the motives within your heart.
5. Take note of what He shows you.
6. Reflect on what you see and experience.
7. If you feel you have had wrong motives, ask for forgiveness, and release your purpose to God.
8. If you feel you have had positive motives, ask God to continue that work in your life.
9. Receive the truth that God will strengthen you to complete His purpose for your life.

28

PRAYER PROMPT

Pray for a close friend or family member who has recently suffered a setback, that God will remind them of their true purpose in life.

29

AUGUST

"I can do all this through him who gives me strength."

PHILIPPIANS 4:13, NIV

AFFIRMATION

No matter what my future holds, or what my purpose will be, I can accomplish anything because God strengthens me.

30
AUGUST

PRAYER PROMPT

Pray for those who must pass exams to get advanced degrees, like a master's or doctorate, that God will give them extraordinary concentration and peace as they pursue their path.

31
AUGUST

END OF THE MONTH PRACTICE

The Feeling of Victory. Make a list of all the major victories God has given you over difficult situations in your life or career. Reflect on those moments of victory: How did they make you feel? Remember how He got you through the difficulties to get to the victories, and how you felt on the other side of it. Now write down your goals for the future. Trust that when God sets your purpose into place, there is nothing that can stop Him.

SEPTEMBER

FAITH

1

SEPTEMBER

PRAYER PROMPT

God, grow my faith so that I can trust you in all circumstances.

2

SEPTEMBER

"And without faith it is impossible to please God, because anyone who comes to him must believe that he exists and that he rewards those who earnestly seek him."

HEBREWS 11:6, NIV

AFFIRMATION

As I believe in God and seek to know Him more, He will be pleased with me.

3

"As Scripture says, 'Anyone who believes in him will never be put to shame.'"

ROMANS 10:11, NIV

MEDITATION

1. Allow yourself the space to slow yourself down and just be.
2. Peacefully bring your hands to prayer. Close your eyes.
3. Pray quietly: "Jesus, I believe in you. I trust that you hold me close."
4. Feel Him sit across from you. Look up into His eyes and allow His words to enter your heart as He says, "If you believe in me, you will never be put to shame. No matter what happens to you, I love you so much."
5. Offer praise to Jesus for taking away all your shame, and for His everlasting presence.

4

PRAYER PROMPT

I pray for my church, that people experience God's love in new ways, and that they grow in their faith.

5

SEPTEMBER

"Yet he did not waver through unbelief regarding the promise of God but was strengthened in his faith and gave glory to God, being fully persuaded that God had power to do what he had promised."

ROMANS 4:20–21, NIV

AFFIRMATION

I believe God has the power to do what He promises, and I am grateful.

6

"Know therefore that the Lord your God is God;
he is the faithful God, keeping his covenant of love
to a thousand generations of those who love him
and keep his commandments."

DEUTERONOMY 7:9, NIV

MEDITATION

1. In peaceful silence, feel the warmth of God's love for you.
2. Sense His presence around you, feel His delight in being in your company.
3. Take a few deep breaths.
4. With each inhale, say to yourself, "God is the loving and faithful God."
5. With each exhale, say to yourself, "He keeps His promises to all generations."
6. Consider a time when God blessed you or your loved ones with an unexpected gift.
7. Thank Him for His faithfulness; be specific with your praise.
8. As you go about your day, choose to experience small blessings as gifts from your faithful and generous Father.

7

PRAYER PROMPT

Heavenly Father, show me ways that you have shown up for me in the past, so that my faith will grow stronger for the future.

8

SEPTEMBER

"For everyone born of God overcomes the world.
This is the victory that has overcome the world, even
our faith. Who is it that overcomes the world?
Only the one who believes that Jesus is the Son of God."

1 JOHN 5:4–5, NIV

AFFIRMATION

I can overcome anything if I believe in Jesus.

9

"Consequently, faith comes from hearing the message, and the message is heard through the word about Christ."

ROMANS 10:17, NIV

MEDITATION

1. Take a deep breath and allow any worries, fears, or anger to leave your body.
2. Now that you feel lighter, tell Jesus something you love about Him.
3. Open your hands with your palms faceup and receive His response with quiet humility.
4. Take another deep breath.
5. As you inhale, say to yourself, "For God so loved the world."
6. As you exhale, say to yourself, "That He gave His one and only Son to die for me."
7. Quietly pray: "God, I believe, and I receive this gift."

10
SEPTEMBER

PRAYER PROMPT

Jesus, I thank you for .... (a person). Through their influence in my life, I have seen what true faith is.

11
SEPTEMBER

"So in Christ Jesus you are all children of God through faith, for all of you who were baptized into Christ have clothed yourselves with Christ."

GALATIANS 3:26–27, NIV

AFFIRMATION

Through my faith in Jesus, I am a child of God.

12

SEPTEMBER

—

"Jesus replied, 'Truly I tell you, if you have faith and do not doubt,
not only can you do what was done to the fig tree,
but also you can say to this mountain, "Go, throw yourself
into the sea," and it will be done. If you believe, you will receive
whatever you ask for in prayer.'"

MATTHEW 21:21–22, NIV

MEDITATION

1. Get on your knees and allow time for your mind to slow down and focus on God.
2. Picture a burden you thought was too big for you or God to handle.
3. Imagine God saying, "If you have faith, I can move mountains."
4. See Jesus by your side and ask Him to help you let go of this burden.
5. Feel His peace flowing through you as you no longer feel weighed down, but instead feel recharged in your body and faith.

13
SEPTEMBER

PRAYER PROMPT

Holy Spirit, lead me to someone who I can encourage, and give me the words to uplift them in faith in their current situation.

14
SEPTEMBER

"He is the Rock, his works are perfect, and all his ways are just. A faithful God who does no wrong, upright and just is he."

DEUTERONOMY 32:4, NIV

AFFIRMATION

God's faithful love for me is perfect.

15

"Whoever believes in me, as Scripture has said, rivers
of living water will flow from within them."

JOHN 7:38, NIV

MEDITATION

1. Close your eyes and imagine the sight and sounds of a clear, beautiful rushing river.
2. See how it flows so effortlessly but brings about so much power and life.
3. See the trees, flowers, and wildlife on the banks of the river thriving from its abundance.
4. Hear Jesus tell you: "Come to me all you who are thirsty. As you believe in me, rivers of living water will flow from within you."
5. Breathe in and say to yourself, "I believe in you, Jesus."
6. Breathe out and say to yourself, "Thank you for quenching my thirst, Lord."
7. Feel the Holy Spirit's presence and peace flow through your thirsty soul, filling you up with His love.

16
SEPTEMBER

PRAYER PROMPT

Jesus, I pray for anyone who is empty today. Will you remind them as they trust in you, that you will fill us up to overflowing?

17
SEPTEMBER

"'Go,' said Jesus, 'your faith has healed you.' Immediately he received his sight and followed Jesus along the road."

MARK 10:52, NIV

AFFIRMATION

I can call on Jesus in faith, and He will see me, heal me, and make me new.

18

"For it is by grace you have been saved, through faith—and this is
not from yourselves, it is the gift of God—not
by works, so that no one can boast."

EPHESIANS 2:8–9, NIV

MEDITATION

1. Let your body relax with your hands facing down.
2. Imagine dropping any vying and striving from your life, right to the floor.
3. Now turn your hands up.
4. Picture Jesus handing you the free gift of paying the price for your sins.
5. Hear Him say, "It is by grace you've been saved, through faith."
6. Accept the gift and tell Jesus: "Thank you for what you've done for me. I believe in you!"
7. Hear Him whisper, "You are my masterpiece. I made you; you can let go of striving for love and approval, because you already have it in me."

19

PRAYER PROMPT

Lord, help me grasp the great extent to which you've saved me, and help me believe deeper in all that you've done for me.

20

SEPTEMBER

"'If you can?' said Jesus. 'Everything is possible for one who believes.' Immediately the boy's father exclaimed, 'I do believe; help me overcome my unbelief!'"

MARK 9:23–24, NIV

AFFIRMATION

I believe in Jesus, who helps me overcome any areas of unbelief in my heart.

21

"Therefore I tell you, whatever you ask for in prayer, believe that you have received it, and it will be yours."

MARK 11:24, NIV

MEDITATION

1. What requests do you have for God today? Pour them all out to Him.
2. Hear Him say, "I love you so much, child. You don't have to be afraid. You can ask me for anything."
3. Sit with Him for a few quiet minutes.
4. Repeat the scripture above to yourself several times, building your faith with each repetition.
5. Say out loud, "I can trust God with the big things and the small things. All He wants me to do is ask Him in faith for what I desire, and He will answer."
6. Thank God for every good gift from Him.

22
SEPTEMBER

PRAYER PROMPT

As my friends, family, and I face hard circumstances, please help us grow our faith in You, Lord. Let us know You are for us and not against us.

23
SEPTEMBER

"For we live by faith, not by sight."

2 CORINTHIANS 5:7, NIV

AFFIRMATION

Many of the most important things in life can't be seen. I will walk in faith knowing Jesus is beside me today.

24

"'But, Lord,' said Martha, the sister of the dead man,
'by this time there is a bad odor, for he has been there
four days.' Then Jesus said, 'Did I not tell you that if you believe, you
will see the glory of God?' When he had said
this, Jesus called in a loud voice, 'Lazarus, come out!'
The dead man came out..."

JOHN 11:39–40, 43, 44, NIV

MEDITATION

1. Take a few deep breaths as you meditate on the scripture above.
2. Ask the Holy Spirit to highlight whatever He needs you to hear.
3. Read the verse slowly and see what stands out to you.
4. Listen for how God wants to grow your faith.
5. End your time by reflecting on the fact Jesus conquered death and *nothing* is too difficult for Him.

25

SEPTEMBER

PRAYER PROMPT

I pray for _____, who is experiencing a hard situation right now. Will you help their faith grow even through this trial, Lord?

26

SEPTEMBER

PRAYER PROMPT

Papa God, I thank you for letting *nothing* separate me from your love. Even in times when I feel faithless, you remain so faithful. Amen.

27

"If we are faithless, he remains faithful, for he cannot disown himself."

2 TIMOTHY 2:13, NIV

MEDITATION

1. Jesus wants to walk beside you today.
2. Sit peacefully.
3. Tell God about the times in your life when it's been hard to trust Him (these can be found in times of worry).
4. Hear Him tell you: "Even when you feel faithless, I will always be faithful to you."
5. Commit to Him the times of worry.
6. Hear Him say, "I am trustworthy to hold all these important things in your life, child."
7. Spend time dwelling on His words of truth and His faithful love.

28

"Jesus said to her, 'I am the resurrection and the life.
The one who believes in me will live, even though they die;
and whoever lives by believing in me will never die.
Do you believe this?'"

JOHN 11:25–26, NIV

AFFIRMATION

*I believe that Jesus conquered
death and that I will be in eternity with Him.*

29

"Trust in the Lord with all your heart and lean not
on your own understanding; in all your ways submit
to him, and he will make your paths straight."

PROVERBS 3:5–6, NIV

AFFIRMATION

I will let Jesus set me in the right destination.

30

SEPTEMBER

END OF THE MONTH PRACTICE

Faith can be made stronger by remembering what God has faithfully done for
you in the past. Try writing prayer requests to God: Start with smaller ones and
then move to larger, more important ones. As God begins to answer them take
notice. As you see the ways that God is answering your prayers, your faith will
grow, and you will see that you can trust Him with bigger and bigger requests.

OCTOBER

GENEROSITY

1

OCTOBER

PRAYER PROMPT

Lord, you are so generous. I praise you for all your amazing gifts!
You give me life, breath, and every other good thing.

2

OCTOBER

"Because of the service by which you have proved yourselves,
others will praise God for the obedience that accompanies your
confession of the gospel of Christ, and for your generosity in
sharing with them and with everyone else."

2 CORINTHIANS 9:13, NIV

AFFIRMATION

*Being generous in service, not just donations,
can make me happier.*

3

OCTOBER

"Give, and it will be given to you. A good measure,
pressed down, shaken together and running over,
will be poured into your lap. For with the measure you use,
it will be measured to you."

LUKE 6:38, NIV

MEDITATION

1. Take a few deep breaths.
2. Picture sitting under a waterfall of God's love.
3. Feel His love continually pouring over your head onto your lap.
4. Ask Jesus to help you think about and see each person today with this amazing abundance of love.
5. Continue to feel the love pouring over you.
6. Ask Jesus, "Help me love like you."

4
OCTOBER

Jesus, help me be generous with my neighbors today. Show me how I can help their needs be met.

5
OCTOBER

"One person gives freely, yet gains even more; another withholds unduly, but comes to poverty. A generous person will prosper; whoever refreshes others will be refreshed."

PROVERBS 11:24–25, NIV

AFFIRMATION

I can't outgive God; the more I give away to others, the more God gives back to me.

6

"You will be enriched in every way so that you can be generous on every occasion, and through us your generosity will result in thanksgiving to God."

2 CORINTHIANS 9:11, NIV

AFFIRMATION

There is no end to the way God keeps enriching my life.

7

OCTOBER

PRAYER PROMPT

Jesus, I pray that I do not have a scarcity mindset. Even when I have little, you can multiple that into a lot. Help me be generous with the people in my life.

8

"For where your treasure is, there your heart will be also."

MATTHEW 6:21, NIV

MEDITATION

1. Take a deep breath and ask God to meet you at this moment.
2. Quietly ask Him, "What things am I treasuring more than you right now? Where am I spending my time away from you?"
3. Close your eyes and take notice of anything that comes into your mind.
4. Bring your hands to prayer and pray to God: "Father, I offer up these things to you."
5. Pressing further in prayer, admit "For where my treasure is, there my heart will be also."
6. Take a moment to picture what the perfect day would look like with you and God.
7. Take to heart how He makes you feel as He spends quality time with you.
8. Commit today to treasuring God more than time or things or anything else.

9

OCTOBER

"Through Jesus, therefore, let us continually offer to God a sacrifice of praise—the fruit of lips that openly profess his name. And do not forget to do good and to share with others, for with such sacrifices God is pleased."

HEBREWS 13:15–16, NIV

MEDITATION

1. Take some deep breaths and stretch your arms as far away from your body as you can.
2. Read through the above scripture slowly, allowing the Holy Spirit to guide you.
3. Tell God what stands out to you.
4. Allow time to quiet your mind and listen to God.
5. Ask Him what good He wants you to do today.
6. Tell Him: "I want to openly profess your name, Jesus. Help me do good and share with others."

10

OCTOBER

PRAYER PROMPT

God, I pray for those who are suffering from hunger or thirst. Please help me and other people meet their needs today.

11

OCTOBER

"Do you still not understand? Don't you remember the five loaves for the five thousand, and how many basketfuls you gathered?"

MATTHEW 16:9, NIV

AFFIRMATION

Put the little you have in God's hands. He can do what no one else can!

12

OCTOBER

"As Jesus looked up, he saw the rich putting their gifts
into the temple treasury. He also saw a poor widow put in
two very small copper coins. 'Truly I tell you,' He said,
'this poor widow has put in more than all the others. All
these people gave their gifts out of their wealth; but
she out of her poverty put in all she had to live on.'"

LUKE 21:1–4, NIV

MEDITATION

1. Relax your body and empty your mind as you reread the above words.
2. Picture being in this scene next to Jesus.
3. Tell Jesus your initial reactions.
4. Who do you relate to in the story?
5. Are there changes you need to make in your life?

13

OCTOBER

PRAYER PROMPT

Father God, help me see others through your lens of love, and be generous to them with whatever gifts you've given me.

14

OCTOBER

"He gives strength to the weary and increases
the power of the weak."

ISAIAH 40:29, NIV

AFFIRMATION

*My weakness put in God's hands
becomes uniqueness for His plans.
His generosity overcomes all.*

15

*"'Bring the whole tithe into the storehouse, that there
may be food in my house. Test me in this,' says the Lord Almighty,
'and see if I will not throw open the floodgates
of heaven and pour out so much blessing that there
will not be room enough to store it.'"*

MALACHI 3:10, NIV

MEDITATION

1. Tighten your hands, then release your grip.
2. Do it again, this time focusing on how it feels to have your hands tight, and then relaxed.
3. As you release your grip, picture your worries about finances dropping out of your hands.
4. Tell Jesus, "I will bring my tithe to you, Jesus. I trust you with my money."
5. Hear Him say, "I will throw open the floodgates of heaven. I will pour out blessing upon blessing on you!"

16

OCTOBER

PRAYER PROMPT

Pray for God to give you the resources to bless someone else financially this month.

17

OCTOBER

"But Zacchaeus stood up and said to the Lord,
'Look, Lord! Here and now I give half of my possessions
to the poor, and if I have cheated anybody out of anything,
I will pay back four times the amount.'"

LUKE 19:8, NIV

AFFIRMATION

*I will give generously today out of
the abundance God gives me.*

18
OCTOBER

"Remember this: Whoever sows sparingly
will also reap sparingly, and whoever sows
generously will also reap generously."

2 CORINTHIANS 9:6, NIV

MEDITATION

1. Close your eyes and meditate on the scripture above.
2. In a whisper, say, "I will reap what I sow."
3. Picture a farmer working in a field.
4. Notice how he tends to his crops, watering them, pulling out weeds, and nurturing the plants until he receives a full harvest.
5. Then picture another farmer who spends no time with his crops; they spring up, then wither fast, leaving no plants to harvest.
6. With these two options before you, which farmer would you rather be?
7. Pray to God: "Father, help me be generous to others in love, so that I may receive Your generosity."

19
OCTOBER

PRAYER PROMPT

God, teach me how to trust you financially, so that I can freely give to others.

20
OCTOBER

"Each of you should give what you have decided in your heart to give, not reluctantly or under compulsion, for God loves a cheerful giver."

2 CORINTHIANS 9:7, NIV

AFFIRMATION

Giving to others is a blessing;
God loves a cheerful giver.

21

"Give generously to them and do so without a grudging heart; then because of this the Lord your God will bless you in all your work and in everything you put your hand to."

DEUTERONOMY 15:10, NIV

MEDITATION

1. Start today with prayer, thanking God for His generosity toward you.
2. Think of something that God has done for you recently that made you feel a little extra love.
3. Pray: "Father, thank you for giving generously to me, without finding fault."
4. Ask Him to help you think of a situation in which you might be able to give generously, with either your time or talent.
5. Picture how you might have an impact with your gift of time or know-how.
6. Plan your day or week accordingly.

22
OCTOBER

PRAYER PROMPT

Father, I thank you for _____ (a person/people). I am so thankful that you brought them into my life, to bless me during a difficult time.

23
OCTOBER

PRAYER PROMPT

Pray for organizations that give food, money, clothing, and shelter to those in need.

24
OCTOBER

"For I was hungry and you gave me something to eat,
I was thirsty and you gave me something to drink, I was a stranger
and you invited me in … The King will reply, 'Truly I tell you,
whatever you did for one of the least of these brothers and sisters
of mine, you did for me.'"

MATTHEW 25:35, 40, NIV

MEDITATION

1. Jesus wants to sit with you today.
2. Slowly read the verse above.
3. Think of a time when your generous help went unnoticed or unacknowledged.
4. Hear God say, "I'm so proud of you, daughter/son. Even if you don't get a thanks from them, please know I see you. Your reward will be great in heaven as you serve others in love."
5. Feel Jesus's love rush over you as you pause in His presence.

25

OCTOBER

"But when you give to the needy, do not let your left hand know what your right hand is doing, so that your giving may be in secret. Then your Father, who sees what is done in secret, will reward you."

MATTHEW 6:3–4, NIV

AFFIRMATION

Giving to others is a blessing even when no one else knows.

26

OCTOBER

"He has shown kindness by giving you rain from heaven and crops in their seasons; he provides you with plenty of food and fills your hearts with joy."

ACTS 14:17, NIV

AFFIRMATION

When I think of God's generosity today, I will remember how well He provides rainwater for crops that feed and nourish our body, the same way His Word feeds and nourishes our soul.

27

"Carry each other's burdens, and in this way you will fulfill the law of Christ."

GALATIANS 6:2, NIV

MEDITATION

1. Ask God to bring someone to your mind who is carrying a burden too big for them to bear.
2. Sit quietly and allow Him the space to answer you.
3. Once you have someone in mind, pray: "God, you tell me to carry other people's burdens, and in doing so I am like Christ. Give me a unique way to do this for this person."
4. Allow God's spirit to inspire you.
5. Finish by praying for the person with the burden.
6. Find a way to reach out to them today.

28
OCTOBER

PRAYER PROMPT

Lord, help me have a generous heart even when I have very little to give. I know you provide all that I will ever need.

29
OCTOBER

"Command them to do good, to be rich in good deeds, and to be generous and willing to share."

1 TIMOTHY 6:18, NIV

AFFIRMATION

The best type of wealth comes from being generous, humbly serving, and sharing with others.

30
OCTOBER

PRAYER PROMPT

Pray for those who have riches in abundance, that they would be compelled to give generously and share with those in need.

31
OCTOBER

END OF THE MONTH PRACTICE

Find a Charity. Spend time this week finding an organization that does work you admire, or that you really believe in. Find a way to reach out and donate in whatever way you feel called to help. Whether it's your time, money, or resources, find a way that works best for your situation. Being generous to others is a great way to give back and be spiritually blessed in the process.

NOVEMBER

THANKFULNESS

1
NOVEMBER

PRAYER PROMPT

Heavenly Father, thank you for each new season of life. I appreciate how you teach me new things no matter what I have going on. Teach my eyes to see all that you do.

2
NOVEMBER

PRAYER PROMPT

God, you've made the heavens and the earth. I give you thanks for everything I can see today. The trees, birds, animals, mountains, stars, rivers...all of it! I praise you for being a wonderful creator.

3
NOVEMBER

—

"Every good and perfect gift is from above, coming
down from the Father of the heavenly lights, who
does not change like shifting shadows."

JAMES 1:17, NIV

MEDITATION

1. Jesus loves this dedicated time with you.
2. Quiet your mind as you sit with Him today.
3. Picture large, beautiful beams of light coming from the sky.
4. Feel the Father of Heavenly Lights shining His love on you.
5. As you breathe in, tell Jesus: "Every good and perfect gift is from you, Lord."
6. As you breathe out, tell Him: "Thank you for being unchangeable, unshakable, and amazing."
7. Spend time meditating on all the good things, small and large, God has made just for you.
8. Tell Jesus how grateful you are for every blessing in your life.
9. Spend some time basking in His goodness.

4

PRAYER PROMPT

Everlasting Father, thank you for all the wonderful people you
have placed in my life. Help me always act in kindness and love
toward them.

5

NOVEMBER

"Devote yourselves to prayer, being watchful and thankful."

COLOSSIANS 4:2, NIV

AFFIRMATION

*Today, I will prayerfully be on the watch for
everyday things to be thankful for, like water
coming out of the tap and eyes that can read.*

6

"Thanks be to God for his indescribable gift!"

2 CORINTHIANS 9:15, NIV

AFFIRMATION

God made me. He chose me. He sent His one and only Son to die for me, and conquered death so I could be with Him for eternity! Thank you, Jesus!

7

NOVEMBER

"And whatever you do, whether in word or deed,
do it all in the name of the Lord Jesus, giving thanks
to God the Father through him."

COLOSSIANS 3:17, NIV

AFFIRMATION

*Everything I do today, I do for Jesus, in
thanksgiving for all He's done for me.*

8

"I will extol the Lord at all times; his praise will always
be on my lips . . . I sought the Lord, and he answered me;
he delivered me from all my fears. Those who look to him
are radiant; their faces are never covered with shame."

PSALM 34:1, 4–5, NIV

MEDITATION

1. Turn one of your hands faceup, and picture God's hand holding yours.
2. Hear Him reassure you, "You can trust me with all your fears, I will take care of you."
3. Picture all your fears being released with each breath.
4. Tell Jesus: "I seek your face, Jesus. I praise you for your goodness."
5. Feel gratitude fill your whole body.
6. Picture your face beaming with light as Jesus says, "Your face will reflect my light. I have stripped all the shame from your life."

9

"For the wages of sin is death, but the gift of God is
eternal life in Christ Jesus our Lord."

ROMANS 6:23, NIV

AFFIRMATION

*Our punishment should be death, but because
of the gift of Jesus we can have eternal life.
I praise Jesus for rescuing me!*

10

NOVEMBER

PRAYER PROMPT

Jesus, I pray for my circle of friends, including _____. You
have made them in your image, and I'm so thankful for them.
Help them know you today, Jesus.

11
NOVEMBER

"Therefore, since we are receiving a kingdom that cannot be shaken, let us be thankful, and so worship God acceptably with reverence and awe, for our 'God is a consuming fire.'"

HEBREWS 12:28–29, NIV

AFFIRMATION

I will worship God today in reverence, knowing that His love and goodness are unshakable!

12
NOVEMBER

PRAYER PROMPT

Mighty Counselor, thank you for caring about my health. Help my spiritual, emotional, physical, and relational health, Lord. I also pray for the health of _____ (a person or group of people).

13
NOVEMBER

"Then I heard every creature in heaven and on earth and under the earth and on the sea, and all that is in them, saying: 'To him who sits on the throne and to the Lamb be praise and honor and glory and power, for ever and ever!'"

REVELATION 5:13, NIV

MEDITATION

1. Raise your hands into the air and take a deep stretch.
2. Picture people from all over the world, and every animal, all praising Jesus.
3. See kings and queens throwing down their crowns as they also surrender all before the King of Kings.
4. Imagine all of you raising your hands together in worship and saying: "All praise, honor, glory, and power are yours Jesus! For ever and ever!"
5. Soak in this moment and experience the majesty of our God.

14

NOVEMBER

"And he took bread, gave thanks and broke it, and
gave it to them, saying, 'This is my body given for you;
do this in remembrance of me.'"

LUKE 22:19, NIV

AFFIRMATION

*I give thanks to Jesus for being
the bread of life! He nourishes my
hunger for a more spiritual life.*

15

"One of them, when he saw he was healed, came back, praising God in a loud voice. He threw himself at Jesus' feet and thanked him—and he was a Samaritan. Jesus asked, 'Were not all ten cleansed? Where are the other nine? Has no one returned to give praise to God except this foreigner?' Then he said to him, 'Rise and go; your faith has made you well.'"

LUKE 17:15–19, NIV

MEDITATION

1. Kneel before Jesus.
2. Read the scripture above again, picturing the scene.
3. Reflect to Jesus on how you relate to the healed lepers who'd failed to give Him thanks.
4. Tell Jesus: "For all the times I've failed to give you thanks, please let me do that now. Thank you, Jesus, for everything, especially ...."
5. Hear Him say, "Rise and go, your faith has made you well."
6. Feel His appreciation enwrap your whole body.

16
NOVEMBER

PRAYER PROMPT

God, I thank you for providing for all my basic needs. I pray that I will always be filled with gratitude for your provisions.

17
NOVEMBER

"For everything God created is good, and nothing is to be rejected if it is received with thanksgiving, because it is consecrated by the word of God and prayer."

1 TIMOTHY 4:4–5, NIV

AFFIRMATION

All that God created is good. I am so thankful for each new blessing He gives me.

18
NOVEMBER

"Rejoice always, pray continually, give thanks in all circumstances; for this is God's will for you in Christ Jesus."

1 THESSALONIANS 5:16–18, NIV

MEDITATION

1. In quiet peace, give thanks to the Lord for today.
2. Repeat the following statements quietly, pausing between each statement, and let the Lord speak life into your body:
   - "I will always rejoice."
   - "I will give thanks in all circumstances."
   - "I will pray continually."
   - "I will be thankful for the little things in my life."
   - "I am so thankful for Jesus."
   - "God's will is for me to be thankful."
3. End your time by thanking God for five things in your life right now.
4. Feel the calm and cool presence of gratefulness pouring over your body.

19
NOVEMBER

PRAYER PROMPT

Heavenly Father, thank you for people who give to others generously, please continue to provide for them so that they can continue to give with a grateful heart.

20
NOVEMBER

"Let us come before him with thanksgiving and extol him with music and song. For the Lord is the great God, the great King above all gods. In his hand are the depths of the earth, and the mountain peaks belong to him."

PSALM 95:2–4, NIV

AFFIRMATION

God is worthy of all our praise.

21
NOVEMBER

"The stone the builders rejected has become the cornerstone; the Lord has done this, and it is marvelous in our eyes. The Lord has done it this very day; let us rejoice today and be glad."

PSALM 118:22–24, NIV

MEDITATION

1. Close your eyes and picture a huge stone wall.
2. Imagine that each stone represents a different piece of your life.
3. You notice there's a hole in the wall that's almost causing it to collapse.
4. Imagine seeing a stone next to you on the ground.
5. You pick up that stone and place it in the hole; it's a perfect fit and holds the wall together.
6. This stone is Jesus. When you are about to fall apart, He holds you together.
7. Thank Jesus today for being there when you need Him.

22
NOVEMBER

PRAYER PROMPT

Father, thank you for providing for me. Help me work hard at all I
do, out of thankfulness for you.

23
NOVEMBER

"… Sing and make music from your heart to the Lord,
always giving thanks to God the Father for everything,
in the name of our Lord Jesus Christ."

EPHESIANS 5:19–20, NIV

AFFIRMATION

*With every fiber of my being,
I give thanks to the Lord.*

24

> "I will give thanks to the Lord because of his righteousness;
> I will sing the praises of the name of the Lord Most High."

PSALM 7:17, NIV

MEDITATION

1. Bow your head and close your eyes in reverence before God.
2. Place your hands in prayer, then pray: "Lord most high, I am so thankful for your righteousness. Thank you for saving me and for loving me. I am humbled to be in your presence, and I thank you for spending time with me."
3. Ask God to draw closer to you, then sit quietly, allowing your senses to feel His presence surrounding you like a warm blanket.
4. Remember a time when you felt that God delighted in you. Thank Him for His love in that moment.

25
NOVEMBER

PRAYER PROMPT

Heavenly Father, thank you for providing me with interests, passions, and hobbies. Help me always glorify you through them.

26
NOVEMBER

"So then, just as you received Christ Jesus as Lord, continue to live your lives in him, rooted and built up in him, strengthened in the faith as you were taught, and overflowing with thankfulness."

COLOSSIANS 2:6–7, NIV

AFFIRMATION

I am thankful to be so rooted in my faith.

27

"Enter his gates with thanksgiving and his courts
with praise; give thanks to him and praise his name.
For the Lord is good and his love endures forever; his faithfulness
continues through all generations."

PSALM 100:4–5, NIV

MEDITATION

1. Take a few deep breaths.
2. Picture a time line with every event in history from the past, the present, and the future.
3. Notice God was there at the beginning, and God is still present at the other end.
4. Let this image soak in. God, who is love, endures forever.
5. With each inhale, say to yourself, "The Lord is good."
6. With each exhale, say to yourself, "His love endures forever."
7. End with a quiet appreciation by saying, "Thank you, God, for the enduring love you are sending me at all times."

28

NOVEMBER

PRAYER PROMPT

Father, I am thankful for _____ (a person, event, or item). Because of your love I get to experience life to its absolute fullest.

29

NOVEMBER

"We always thank God for all of you and continually mention you in our prayers."

1 THESSALONIANS 1:2, NIV

AFFIRMATION

Praying for others, and thanking God for them, helps me appreciate and love them even more.

30

END OF THE MONTH PRACTICE

The Grateful Five Challenge.

1. Tell God five things you are thankful for since you woke up this morning.
2. Offer Jesus five things you are thankful for as you start each prayer time today.
3. Today, tell five people why and how you are thankful for them. It can be in person, over the phone, or in a note, email, or text.
4. As you go about your day, reflect on five things in your life for which you are grateful.
5. End your day by telling God five things you were grateful for today.

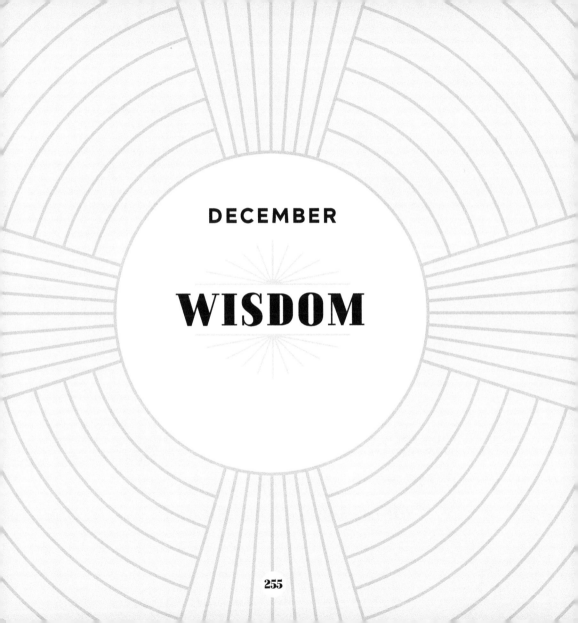

DECEMBER

WISDOM

1

DECEMBER

PRAYER PROMPT

Father, give me wisdom over my finances so that I can make wise decisions, receive your blessings, and have a secure future.

2

DECEMBER

"Who is wise and understanding among you?
Let them show it by their good life, by deeds done
in the humility that comes from wisdom."

JAMES 3:13, NIV

AFFIRMATION

*Wisdom makes me humble and
allows me to live a good life.*

3

"For the Lord gives wisdom; from his mouth
come knowledge and understanding."

PROVERBS 2:6, NIV

MEDITATION

1. In quiet surrender, slowly move your arms into a receiving posture, as if you are receiving a gift.
2. Speaking in a gentle whisper, say, "The Lord gives wisdom."
3. Whisper again, "From God's mouth comes knowledge and understanding."
4. Picture Him placing wisdom into your hands, as if it were a weapon for battle or a tool for construction.
5. Allow His understanding to supersede your own; trust that He knows all.
6. Silently pray: "Father, today I choose to trust in Your wisdom. Please guide my decisions as I go about my day and week."

4
DECEMBER

PRAYER PROMPT

Pray for those who work in the court system, that they act in wisdom, and judge fairly over their cases.

5
DECEMBER

"Be very careful, then, how you live—not as unwise but as wise, making the most of every opportunity, because the days are evil."

EPHESIANS 5:15–16, NIV

AFFIRMATION

Evil can overtake me, so I must act wisely and make the most of opportunities.

6

> "How much better to get wisdom than gold,
> to get insight rather than silver!"

PROVERBS 16:16, NIV

MEDITATION

1. Close your eyes and picture a large room filled with treasure.
2. The walls are made of pure gold, stacks of silver coins cover the room, and precious stones glisten with beauty and wonder.
3. In the middle of the room is an old chest. You walk over and open it. Inside you find wisdom and insight, which can give you more understanding than anyone else in the world.
4. You have the choice to take the treasure or what's inside the chest.
5. Meditate on the above verse and ask God to give you strength to choose His wisdom and insight, even over all the riches on earth.

7

PRAYER PROMPT

Father God, give me wisdom so that I can provide for my family and love them the way they deserve to be loved.

8

DECEMBER

"Fools give full vent to their rage, but the wise bring calm in the end."

PROVERBS 29:11, NIV

AFFIRMATION

If I give in to my anger I can act out in rage, but if I act in wisdom I can bring calmness to my life and the lives of others.

9

"The fear of the Lord is the beginning of knowledge,
but fools despise wisdom and instruction."

PROVERBS 1:7, NIV

MEDITATION

1. Begin today with quiet stillness as you sit in God's presence.
2. Repeat these words: "The fear of the Lord is the beginning of knowledge."
3. Ask God to give you wisdom, that in fearing Him, His truth would rest on you.
4. Picture His wisdom pouring over your shoulders. Sense His wisdom pressing on you.
5. Get on your knees and ask God to reveal to you a way He has been trying to impart His wisdom recently.
6. Patiently wait for His response, noting anything that comes to mind.
7. Finish your time today by placing your worries and fears into His hands and receiving instruction and truth from His hands in return.

10
DECEMBER

Jesus, teach me how to grasp your wisdom and make good choices in my life, trusting that you are with me every step of the way.

11
DECEMBER

"Therefore everyone who hears these words of mine and puts them into practice is like a wise man who built his house on the rock."

MATTHEW 7:24, NIV

AFFIRMATION

*If I follow Jesus and His teachings,
I will have a strong foundation.*

12

"For the foolishness of God is wiser than human wisdom, and the weakness of God is stronger than human strength."

1 CORINTHIANS 1:25, NIV

MEDITATION

1. Take a moment and picture the smartest person you've ever heard of or known.
2. Then picture the strongest person you've ever heard of or known.
3. What makes that first person smart? What makes the second person strong?
4. Let those images sink in and say the verse above out loud.
5. Then pray: "God, you are wiser and stronger than me. Give me a heart of understanding and help me rely on you for strength."
6. Finish with a time of worship for the King of the Universe.

13

PRAYER PROMPT

Heavenly Father, help me read your word with fresh eyes each day so that I can learn more from you and gain your infinite wisdom.

14
DECEMBER

"Even fools are thought wise if they keep silent, and discerning if they hold their tongues."

PROVERBS 17:28, NIV

AFFIRMATION

It's smarter to listen and hold my tongue than to speak without thinking.

15

DECEMBER

"Do not conform to the pattern of this world, but be transformed by the renewing of your mind. Then you will be able to test and approve what God's will is—his good, pleasing and perfect will."

ROMANS 12:2, NIV

MEDITATION

1. Take a few deep breaths to begin your time today.
2. With each inhale, say to yourself, "Father, transform my mind."
3. With each exhale, say to yourself, "So I can know your perfect will."
4. Sitting in silence, begin to think truths about God.
5. Allow your mind to fix solely on the truths told in scripture about God.
6. If a lie comes up about you or God, say, "Father, renew my mind."
7. Feel His presence around you, sensing the transformation of your mind as you abide in the presence of God the Father.

16
DECEMBER

Lord, would you please give me wisdom over all my relationships? I pray specifically for my relationship with _____.

17
DECEMBER

"If any of you lacks wisdom, you should ask God,
who gives generously to all without finding fault,
and it will be given to you."

JAMES 1:5, NIV

AFFIRMATION

*I will ask God for wisdom in small and
big decisions today, knowing
He gives freely and generously to me.*

18
DECEMBER

"Ah, Sovereign Lord, you have made the heavens and the earth by your great power and outstretched arm. Nothing is too hard for you."

JEREMIAH 32:17, NIV

MEDITATION

1. Take a few deep breaths as you place your worries and life before Jesus.
2. Reread the above scripture, taking in every word.
3. Imagine, vividly, God creating the heavens and the earth.
4. Experience the majesty and power of who He is.
5. Consider all that Jesus has done in your life, and in the life of the world.
6. Tell Jesus: "Nothing is too hard for you."
7. Repeat that phrase over any situation you're facing.
8. Be filled with the wisdom, courage, and peace of who Christ is in your life.

19
DECEMBER

PRAYER PROMPT

Holy Spirit, I ask for wisdom in choosing friendships. Please also give me courage and direction to make wise choices while I'm with my friends.

20
DECEMBER

"Do not be wise in your own eyes; fear the Lord and shun evil."

PROVERBS 3:7, NIV

AFFIRMATION

I will turn from evil today. I won't trust my own heart, but instead trust in God's wise guidance.

21
DECEMBER

"Whoever speaks on their own does so to gain personal glory, but he who seeks the glory of the one who sent him is a man of truth; there is nothing false about him."

JOHN 7:18, NIV

MEDITATION

1. The Holy Spirit wants to speak to you today.
2. Hand over anything for which you seek wisdom this week.
3. Spend time in complete silence, listening for the Holy Spirit to speak to you.
4. Journal anything you might hear.
5. If the answer aligns with scripture, ask Jesus, "Help me grasp this wisdom. Lord, help me be a person filled with your truth."

22
DECEMBER

"But make up your mind not to worry beforehand how you will defend yourselves. For I will give you words and wisdom that none of your adversaries will be able to resist or contradict."

LUKE 21:14–15, NIV

MEDITATION

1. Close your eyes as you picture Jesus's hand gently on your cheek.
2. With each breath, feel a release of the things on your mind.
3. Let the tension in your body release as you hear Jesus remind you that you don't need to figure everything out.
4. Tell God: "I trust you to give me wisdom."
5. Hear the Holy Spirit whisper: "I will give you the words you need when you trust me."
6. Reread the scripture, and let it soak into your soul so it's ready to be pulled forth when you need it next.

23
DECEMBER

"Be wise in the way you act toward outsiders; make
the most of every opportunity. Let your conversation
be always full of grace, seasoned with salt, so that
you may know how to answer everyone."

COLOSSIANS 4:5–6, NIV

AFFIRMATION

*God will give me wisdom and
grace in my conversations
with others, in order to share
His love with them.*

24

"When they saw the star, they were overjoyed. On coming to the house, they saw the child with his mother Mary, and they bowed down and worshiped him. Then they opened their treasures and presented him with gifts of gold, frankincense and myrrh."

MATTHEW 2:10–11, NIV

MEDITATION

1. Take time to read all of Matthew 2 and put yourself in the story of Jesus's birth.
2. Picture the three wise men traveling not to see baby Jesus, but to meet a King who would change history.
3. Say to Jesus, "You are the King above all kings. I give you my best today, Lord."
4. Feel the surrender of giving your life as an offering to Jesus.

25

PRAYER PROMPT

Jesus, thank you for being born to us to save the world. Help me grasp how you're the God of all wisdom, honor, and glory.

26

DECEMBER

"...Not many of you were wise by human standards; not many were influential; not many were of noble birth. But God chose the foolish things of the world to shame the wise; God chose the weak things of the world to shame the strong."

1 CORINTHIANS 1:26–27, NIV

AFFIRMATION

Jesus arrived in the world as a lowly child to show the world what true riches are.

27
DECEMBER

PRAYER PROMPT

Great Physician, I ask for the wisdom to make good choices in what I eat, the motivation to stay active, and the health of my body, mind, soul, and spirit. I also pray for wisdom in the area of health for _____.

28
DECEMBER

PRAYER PROMPT

Mighty Counselor, I ask you for wisdom to set healthy boundaries in my life. I specifically ask for help with/about _____.

29

"So God said to him, 'Since you have asked for this and not
for long life or wealth for yourself, nor have asked for
the death of your enemies but for discernment in
administering justice, I will do what you have asked.
I will give you a wise and discerning heart …'"

1 KINGS 3:11–12, NIV

AFFIRMATION

*God offers discerning wisdom when I ask Him
to help me love and lead others well.*

30
DECEMBER

PRAYER PROMPT

Jesus, my Savior, let me look at you with awe and wonder all the days of my life. I pray you continue to give me your wisdom, so I can love all those around me.

31
DECEMBER

END OF THE MONTH PRACTICE

Seeking God's Wisdom over Human Wisdom. As many times as you can this week, ask God to give you His wisdom when making decisions. Listen for a response, and make sure it's backed by the character of God and His word. Be obedient to His answer, even if it's contrary to popular opinion or human wisdom. Keep growing this muscle of trusting His voice for the wisdom in your life this week and try to take it with you throughout the rest of your life.

Resources

Stefanie and Caleb Rouse

StefanieRouse.com

Instagram:
@stefanie.rouse
@calebjasonrouse

TikTok:
@StefanieandCaleb

Youtube:
Stefanie and Caleb

Our own website is full of resources to deepen your faith and your relationship with God and others. You can find ebooks, guides, and blog posts about experiencing life to its fullest, with Jesus at the steering wheel.

Church Home Guided Prayers

Churchome.org/guidedprayers

Led by Pastors Judah and Chelsea Smith, this app is a great resource for starting off your day with an audio-guided prayer.

5-Minute Couple's Devotional: 150 Days of Love, Reflection, and Prayer **by Jake Morrill**

This Christian couples' devotional helps both new and lifelong partners connect with each other more deeply through guided conversation and prayer.

52-Week Devotional Journal for Women: Prompts and Prayers to Reflect and Connect with God **by Deb Wolf**

Each week in this devotional journal for women begins with a Scripture passage and a unique reflection. Then, four succinct but stirring prompts give you an opportunity to journal on your life, faith, and relationship with God.

Strength in Faith Devotional: A 52-Week Inspirational Book for Men **by Brandan Robertson**

Each week in this devotional begins with a Scripture reading and accompanying essay. Explore themes like "The Forgiveness Factor," "Wage Peace," "The Comparison Trap," and "Servant Leadership" to guide you through issues at work, relationships, and home.

YouVersion Bible App
YouVersion.com

This amazing resource is for all ages and stages. It offers guided prayer, daily devotional content, and a compelling video series to deepen your faith and prayer life.

Scripture Index

Acknowledgments

Thank you Jesus for being our Savior, Redeemer, and friend. Thank you to our family and friends for believing in us, praying for us, and supporting us. Thank you to our followers and online community—you encourage us everyday. Thank you to the person reading this—you are loved beyond measure! Thank you Caleb, for being my partner in life and in writing this book; you are my hero. Thank you Stefanie, for being my best friend and for encouraging me daily; you are the love of my life.

About the Authors

 **Caleb** and **Stefanie Rouse** cherish being married and working together to share the love of Jesus. They are relationship mentors, authors, and digital creators. With Stefanie's master's in marriage and family therapy with a focus on theology and Caleb's master's in education, they are passionate about empowering others to walk in their God given potential and have been doing so for over a decade. With a combined platform of almost half a million, their mission is to pour into people's lives in the areas of faith and marriage and share everyday trials and triumphs of life.